A CENTURY OF GREAT
AFRICAN-AMERICANS

A CENTURY OF GREAT AFRICAN-AMERICANS

ALISON MUNDY SCHWARTZ

GRAMERCY BOOKS
New York

This 1999 edition is published by Gramercy Books™, an imprint of Random House Value Publishing, Inc. 201 East 50th Street, New York, N.Y. 10022.

Gramercy Books™ and design are trademarks of Random House Value Publishing, Inc.

Random House
New York • Toronto • London • Sydney • Auckland
http://www.randomhouse.com/

Designed by Robert Yaffe

Printed and bound in the United States of America.

Library of Congress Cataloging–in–Publication Data

Schwartz, Alison Mundy, 1957-
    A century of great African Americans / Alison Mundy Schwartz.
    p.   cm.
    ISBN 0-517-20724-9 (hc)
    1. Afro-Americans Biography Dictionaries.   2. Afro-Americans-
-History—20th century Dictionaries.   I. Title.
E185.96.S354   1999
973'.0496073—dc21   99-20451
                                            CIP

ISBN 0-517-20724-9

8 7 6 5 4 3

CONTENTS

INTRODUCTION

ACENTURY OF AFRICAN-AMERICANS celebrates the contributions that black Americans have made throughout the twentieth century.

Today, there are many African-American heroes, from Muhammed Ali to Martin Luther King, Jr.; from Oprah Winfrey to Bill Cosby, Michael Jordan, and Tiger Woods. But it was not always so. Lack of education, opportunity, and recognition as people instead of as slaves kept the many inventions, ideas, and cultural gifts of blacks totally hidden from public knowledge. There were the occasional exceptions, such as Bishop Henry McNeal Turner, appointed by President Abraham Lincoln as the first black chaplain in the U.S. Army; and Frederick Douglass, the most powerful spokesman for blacks in the period of the Civil War who later ran for vice-president on the Equal Rights Party ticket; and Harriet Tubman, leader of the Underground Railroad who is credited with helping more than 300 slaves to freedom.

But it was not until the early years of the twentieth century that true progress began in terms of education and increased opportunity, even though repression still existed. African-Americans fought particularly hard for the improvement of their people through politics and government. The National Association for the Advancement of Colored People (NAACP) and The National Urban League were at the vanguard of organizations dedicated to creating change in the national conscience as they helped black Americans in their struggle for civil rights. By the end of World War I, the black population in America had a presence in every aspect of life. The Harlem Renaissance was flourishing with artists, musicians, and poets gaining recognition. Fletcher Henderson and Louis Armstrong brought jazz to Broadway. Countee Cullen and Arna Bontemps wrote poetry. "Bojangles" Bill Robinson, the Mills Brothers, Ethel Waters thrilled audiences. Langston Hughes began his enduring literary career. The 1920s were rich with talent, and at last, African-Americans were achieving their well-deserved recognition even while their civil rights suffered pitifully. For all the glory of a Marian Anderson, a Duke Ellington, a Paul Robeson, the words of Marc Connelly's "The Green Pastures," inequality reigned, the Ku Klux Klan tormented, and African-Americans still had not taken their rightful place in American society.

World War II brought further change—on the battlefield and off, with people like Joe Louis, Lionel Hampton, Jesse Owens and the infamous 1936 Olympic Games in Berlin. The 1950s brought more change still—to the public's awareness of the outstanding contributions of such African-Americans as Gwendolyn Brooks, Jackie Robinson, Ralph Bunche, Frank Yerby, Ralph Ellison, Lena Horne, Dorothy Dandridge, Carl Rowan, Althea Gibson—but segregation, prejudice, and repression continued to plague the nation. Although school desegregation started to become headline news in the mid-1950s, it took people like the Reverend Ralph D. Abernathy, the Reverend Martin Luther King, Jr.,

Rosa Parks, James Meredith, Medgar W. Evers, and a lot of bloodshed as well as many more years—well into the 1960s—before the indignity of separate bathrooms, separate water fountains, and separate seating ended and full school integration became a day-to-day reality for African-Americans.

Today, the names of African-Americans make up a sizable portion of any list of significant contributors to the twentieth century. Names like General Colin Powell, Justice Clarence Thomas, Coretta Scott King, Barbara Jordan, Shirley Chisholm; Evelyn Ashford and Arthur Ashe. The Reverend Jesse Jackson and Benjamin Hooks. Quincy Jones and Robert L. Johnson. Debi Thomas and Carl Lewis. Willie Mays and Jessye Norman. James Earl Jones and Gregory Hines. No aspect of life—for all Americans—is without the influence of African-Americans, achieving a recognition well-deserved and too long overdue.

Alison Mundy Schwartz

A

HANK AARON

America's all time leading home run hitter, Henry Louis ("Hank") Aaron was born in Mobile, Alabama on February 5, 1934. At the time he was growing up, Mobile was a strongly segregated community. Because his high school didn't have a baseball team, Aaron's first experience with organized baseball was playing on a sandlot team called the Pritchett Athletics. By junior year of high school, he was playing part-time with the Mobile Black Bears, and at the age of 17, in 1951, he signed his first professional contract for $200 a month with the Indianapolis Clowns, a Negro League team with a strong following in the African-American community. At this point Aaron still had to be taught to bat correctly. A quick learner, in his first season he went on to lead the Negro League with a batting average of .467.

Hank Aaron broke Babe Ruth's home run record.

In 1952, Aaron's contract was purchased by the National League Braves, to play for their minor league team in Jacksonville. Again, his .362 batting average led the South Atlantic League, and in 1954, at the age of twenty, Hank was promoted to the major league Milwaukee Braves, where he began his brilliant career.

Three years later, he was named the National League's MVP, and led his team to a world championship. He hit .393 in the World Series including three home runs to lead all batters. Aaron hit home runs in two of the twenty-four All-Star Games in which he played, homered in all three playoff games in 1969, and amassed a lifetime World Series average of .364. During his career, Aaron hit more home runs than anyone else in the history of baseball. In 1974 he broke the home run record previously held by Babe Ruth, with his career 715th "round-tripper." He completed his career in 1976 with a total of 755 home runs, having won the home run and RBI crowns four times each, and was named to 20 consecutive All-Star teams. In 1982, Aaron was elected into the Baseball Hall of Fame.

KAREEM ABDUL-JABBAR

Born on April 16, 1947 and growing up in New York City, Lew Alcindor established himself as a "powerhouse" by the time he was playing high school basketball, leading his team to 71 straight victories. Recruited heavily by the top colleges, he went on to play forward at UCLA, where he quickly became known as the premiere center in the United States. During his three years as a varsity player, Alcindor led UCLA to three NCAA championships, where he earned MVP all three years. In 1968 he converted to Islam and changed his name to Kareem Abdul-Jabbar, which translates as "generous and powerful servant of Allah."

Drafted as a first pick by the NBA's Milwaukee Bucks in 1969, he signed a contract for more than $1,000,000. In 1970 he won the league's MVP and Rookie of the Year awards. The following year he led the Milwaukee Bucks to their first world championship. Known for his fabled "sky hook" shot, perhaps the most powerful in the game, he was traded to the Los Angeles Lakers just before the 1975 season. Abdul-Jabbar continued his remarkable career with the Lakers, leading the team to five NBA championships in nine years. For the ten years he was with the team he scored 10 or more points in every game, at total of 38,387, more than any other player in the history of the NBA. After his retirement in 1990, he formed a jazz record label and pursued a career as an actor. Kareem Abdul-Jabbar's autobiography, *Giant Steps*, was published in 1985.

RALPH D. ABERNATHY

Born in 1926, Ralph Abernathy was educated in Alabama, he earned his bachelor's and master's degrees, and was ordained in the Baptist ministry in 1948. In 1951, while serving as minister at the First Baptist Church in Montgomery, Abernathy met and became close friends with Dr. Martin Luther King, who was the reverend of Montgomery's Dexter Avenue Baptist Church. Together they organized the Montgomery Bus Boycott, the success of which led to the creation of the Southern Negro Leaders Conference, later changed to the Southern Christian Leadership Conference (SCLC).

Reverend Abernathy headed the SCLC from the time of Martin Luther King's death in 1968 until 1977, when he resigned to run for congress (unsuccessfully). Afterward, he returned to Atlanta where he devoted himself full time to West Hunter Street Baptist Church, where he had been pastor since 1961. During the latter part of his life, he became more conservatively politically, alienating some of his fellow civil rights leaders by endorsing Ronald Reagan for president. When his autobiography, *And the Walls Came Tumbling Down*, was published, he drew further criticism from black leaders for confirming rumors of Martin Luther King's adulterous affairs, as well as for his conservative political stances. He died of a heart attack in 1990.

Ralph Abernathy testifying before a Senate Committee in March 1968.

ALVIN AILEY

The Alvin Ailey American Dance Theater, founded in 1958, is among the world's most renowned repertory dance companies. Initially the troupe performed at the 92nd Street YM-YMHA in New York City, drawing rave reviews from critics. Ailey's intense, athletic dance style and creative expression achieved a new artistic perspective on the African-American experience. Many of his major works portrayed themes pertaining to black culture. His most famous work, *Revelations*, which became the signature dance of the AAADT, drew on Ailey's childhood experiences in the Baptist church. *Revelations* explored themes such as group prayer, baptism, private communion and the bond between preacher and congregation. By the time Ailey stopped performing to devote himself to running the dance company in 1965, the AAADT had gained a world wide audience. In 1976, Ailey received the NAACP's Spingarn Medal in recognition of his work, and in 1988 he was honored at the Kennedy Center. Following his death in 1991, the company was taken over by artistic director Judith Jamison, a star dancer with AAADT from 1965–1980. The Alvin Ailey American Dance Theater continues as one of the world's greatest dancing ensembles, a living tribute to Ailey's vision and success.

Alvin Ailey Dance Theater celebrated its 40th anniversary in 1999.

MARGARET WALKER ALEXANDER

Born Margaret Abigail Walker in 1915, Margaret W. Alexander began writing poetry at the age of 15, and went on to earn a BA from Northwestern University and an MA from University of Iowa in 1940. Her literary career soared in 1942 when she became the first black writer to win the Yale Series of Younger Poets Competition for her poem "For My People," published in a collection of the same name. In 1966 her best-selling novel, *Jubilee*, which told the life story of a slave and a white plantation owner in Civil War times, was described by the *New York Times Book Review* as, "chronicling the triumph of a free spirit over many kinds of bondage." After receiving critical acclaim for *Jubilee*, Walker returned to writing poetry, conducting research, teaching and promoting the causes of African-Americans.

MUHAMMED ALI

Muhammed Ali, shown here in 1989.

Born Cassius Marcellus Clay on January 17, 1942 in Louisville, Kentucky, Muhammed Ali grew up in a poor family. He was introduced to boxing at the age of twelve when his bicycle was stolen outside a community recreation center. The policeman who helped him recover the bike also taught boxing, and invited Ali to join his class. Ali claims he started boxing because he thought it was "the quickest way for black people to make it."

After winning the gold medal at the 1960 Olympics, Cassius Clay turned pro. Three years later he created a storm of controversy by converting to the Nation of Islam, a sect that denounces boxing, and changing his name to Muhammed Ali. In 1964 he won the World Heavyweight Title in a knockout match with Sonny Liston. Nine more successful title defenses followed before Ali stirred up controversy once again. This time it was due to his refusal to serve when he was called to the draft in 1967, using his association with the Black Muslims to justify his conscientious objector status.

Stripped of his heavyweight title and banned from boxing for the three years it took to overturn his five-year prison sentence, Ali became an icon to the Peace movement, black urban poor and Third World. His refusal to conform to the draft regulations became associated with much larger social change in America. Vindicated by the Supreme Court in 1970, Ali spent the next three years working his way up to another shot at the title. He amazed the world and regained the crown by defeating George Foreman in a knockout fight on October 30, 1974, which took place in Zaire. A 4-1 underdog at ring time, Ali used his brains and speed to exhaust his stronger, younger opponent. He went on to win three more championship fights against Chuck Wepner, Ron Lyle and Joe Bugner, until he finally lost the crown in 1981 against Canadian heavyweight Trevor Burbick.

Ali is described by sport sociologist Harry Edwards as "probably the single greatest athletic figure of this century in terms of the black community, largely because he turned around the image of the black athlete." He is also well known for his boastful pronouncements, usually delivered as a rhyme or epigram. His self-descriptive phrase, "Float like a butterfly, sting like a bee," became an instantly recognizable, favorite " Ali-ism."

More than just a legendary boxer, Ali is a cultural phenomenon. He has not only changed the world of heavyweight boxing, but also had an enormous impact on the way people view race, religion and civil disobedience. Today he dedicates himself to helping black people everywhere, and places a special emphasis on setting a good example for black youth.

MARIAN ANDERSON

Born February 17, 1902, Marian Anderson's musical talent became evident early, when as a choirgirl in her church in Philadelphia, she displayed an unusual vocal range, often singing soprano, alto, tenor and bass. At the age of nineteen she began studying with Giuseppe Boghettti, who remained her voice teacher for many years. After a fiasco debut solo appearance at Town Hall in New York City in 1922, Anderson gave up hope for a musical career. However, under the intensive tutelage of Boghetti, she won a vocal competition in 1925, which included a solo appearance with the New York Philharmonic.

After studying music and touring Europe in the late 1920's and early 30's, Anderson made a second appearance at Town Hall in 1935, with a very different result. The critical acclaim she received led to more concert appearances throughout the U.S. and Europe.

In 1939, Anderson became the center of a storm of controversy when the Daughters of the American Revolution refused to allow her to sing in a performance at Constitution Hall because of her skin color. First lady Eleanor Roosevelt resigned from the DAR and arranged for Anderson to sing at Lincoln Memorial later that year for an audience of 75,000. In 1955, Anderson made history when she became the first African-American soloist at the Metropolitan Opera House. A State Department tour took her around the world in 1957, and in 1958 Anderson was named to the United States delegation to the United Nations. In 1965 she ended her formal singing career, and received several honors and awards including a Congressional Gold medal in 1978. Marian Anderson died in 1993.

LOUIS ARMSTRONG

Born in 1900, in New Orleans, Louis Armstrong was one of the most durable and influential jazz artists of all

Louis Armstrong thrilled audiences for four decades.

time. He grew up poor, and when he was sent to the Waif's Home for boys as a teenager for firing a pistol in the streets, the bandmaster of the Home taught him to read music and play the coronet and the bugle. By the time he was released from the home eighteen months later, he was leading the band. This began a long career for Armstrong who started playing with Dixieland bands in New Orleans, the roots of a sound which later became known as "Jazz." His mentor was Joe Oliver, one of New Orleans' finest trumpet players; Armstrong followed him to Chicago to play in "King Oliver's" creole jazz band.

By 1924 Armstrong had switched from cornet to the trumpet and was also singing, the combo which later became his trademark. A dynamic performer, Armstrong thrilled audiences with his distinctive style and rasping voice. When he began to move away from his Dixieland sound toward more popular, commercial tunes, his new style was copied by white musicians who formed "Big Bands" and "Swing Bands" that were based on Armstrong's sounds.

In 1932, he headlined the show at the London Palladium, where he acquired the stage name "Satchmo," an accidental contraction of one of his childhood nicknames, "Satchel-mouth." Armstrong's enormous popularity led to stage performances on Broadway, world tours, a movie career, and television appearances. In 1964, his recording of "Hello Dolly" hit number one on the charts. Armstrong died in 1971.

MAYA ANGELOU

Born Marguerite Johnson on April 28, 1928 in St. Louis, Missouri, Maya Angelou was sent to live in Arkansas with her grandmother after her parents divorced when she was three years old. Living in a segregated community in the deep south during the depression was a struggle, but Angelou found support and an appreciation of her black heritage from her grandmother and through her church community. At age eight she was sent back to St. Louis to live with her mother. She experienced a tragedy, which destroyed her spirit and shaped her outlook on the adult world: she was raped by her mother's boyfriend.

Angelou went on to mother a child out of wedlock at the age of sixteen, experience a brief stint with prostitution, work as a waitress, and cook before she began her performing career with dancing jobs in bars.

Maya Angelou speaking in March 1996.

From there she developed more opportunities to perform, and in 1954 toured the world with the black opera *Porgy and Bess*. Returning to the United States, she appeared in various plays, including the 1960 off-Broadway production of *The Blacks*. In the same year she co-wrote and performed Cabaret for Freedom with Godfrey Cambridge, a benefit for the Southern Christian Leadership Conference. Angelou moved to Egypt in 1961, where she became the editor of the *Arab Observer*. Later, in Ghana, she worked at the University of Ghana's School of Music and Drama and became a feature editor of *African Review*.

When Angelou returned to the United States, she taught at UCLA, continued her acting career, and began to publish books, including her autobiography, *I Know Why the Caged Bird Sings*. She has also produced many volumes of poetry which focus on the black experience and blacks in society, and further works of her autobiography in which are considered major contributions to American literature and black literature in particular. In addition, Angelou has written screenplays and theatrical plays. Her performance in Alex Haley's *Roots*, in 1977, earned her an Emmy nomination; and in 1979 her autobiography was made into a television movie, for which she wrote the script and music. In 1993 when she was invited to perform by Bill Clinton, she became the first black woman to speak at a presidential inauguration. Angelou's delivery of her poem "On the Pulse of the Morning" mesmerized the audience and spoke to the entire country about diversity in our culture and working together to create a better future.

ARTHUR ASHE

Ashe on court at Wimbledon in 1968.

Perhaps one of the most respected players in the history of tennis, Arthur Ashe made history as the first black man to win a grand slam tennis tournament when he took the men's singles title at the U.S. Open in 1968.

Born in Richmond, Virginia in 1943, of a diverse ethnic background that included American Indian and Mexican as well as African-American, Ashe began playing tennis at the age of seven.

He started winning tournaments in 1955 and in 1962 became the fifth ranked junior player in the U.S. In 1963 he was named to the Davis Cup team and won 27 out of 32 Davis Cup matches over the next fifteen years. Ashe turned professional in 1969, and became the first black man to win the Wimbledon Singles when he beat

Jimmy Connors in 1975, which made him the first African-American ever to be ranked number one nationally. He won three of the four Grand Slam Tournaments: The U.S. Open, the Australian Open and Wimbledon, and shared the fourth Grand Slam event, the French Open.

During his rise in the tennis world, Ashe remained active in human rights and political issues. He had an active role in having South Africa banned from Davis Cup play, and further protested apartheid by chairing the TransAfrica Forum, and helping to found Artists and Athletes Against Apartheid, an organization that put pressure on South Africa.

Plagued with grave health problems throughout his adult life, Ashe suffered a heart attack in 1979, forc-

ing his retirement from professional tennis at the age of 36. In April of 1992 he was diagnosed with AIDS, contracted through an earlier blood transfusion. In his memoirs, Ashe refers to his illness as "The Beast in the Jungle," and writes, "the news that I had AIDS hit me hard, but did not knock me down." He remarked that handling AIDS paled next to the pain of growing up black in America.

Although he was initially uncomfortable being railroaded into becoming a spokesperson in the war on AIDS, he became an active advocate for increased government funding for AIDS research, and began a $5 million fund-raising campaign. He went on to establish the Arthur Ashe Foundation to facilitate combating the disease. In his memoir, *Days of Grace*, he wrote, "Talking to audiences about AIDS has become in some respects the most important function of my life."

Despite his enormous contribution to combatting AIDS, he was far more interested in fighting for human rights. One of the happiest days of his life came later in 1992, after his diagnosis. He flew to Washington to protest the U.S. immigration policy toward Haitians, and was arrested. Of the experience, Ashe said that night, "It does wonders for your outlook. I'm sure it released a torrent of endorphins. Marching in a protest is a liberating experience. It's one of the great moments you can have in your life."

Ashe was a rare kind of sports hero, an example of what to do when the playing stops. A devoted family man, Ashe left behind his wife, Jean and daughter, Camera, when he died of AIDS related pneumonia in 1993 at the age of 49.

EVELYN ASHFORD

During her long career as a world-class sprinter, Evelyn Ashford was a member of fifteen U.S. national teams, including five Olympic teams. Born April 15, 1957 in Shreveport, Louisiana, Ashford began her athletic career in high school, serving as co-captain of the boys' track team. She became one of the first women to receive an athletic scholarship from UCLA, and dominated the women's 60-yard and 100- and 200-meter dashes during the late 1970's. Competing in her first Olympics in 1976, Ashford came in fifth in the 100 meter. She went on to win AIAW championships in 1977 and 1978, was a surprise double champion in sprints at the 1979 World Cup meet, and won a place on the 1980 Olympic team. Unable to compete in the 1980 summer Olympics in Moscow due to the U.S. boycott, she set her sights on 1984 games. She again won both short sprints at the 1981 World Cup championships, and despite continuing problems with a hamstring injury, won her first gold medal in the 100-meter at the 1984 Olympics. Two weeks later she brought home a second gold as a member of the 4 by 100 relay team.

After giving birth to a daughter in 1985, Ashford returned to training and won the 100-meter at the 1986 Goodwill Games. She once again made the Olympic team in 1988, winning both gold and silver medals. In 1992, at the age of 35, Evelyn Ashford, "The Grand Old Lady of Track," won her fourth and final Olympic gold medal as a member of the sprint relay team.

PEARL BAILEY

Born in 1918 in Newport News, Virginia, singer and actress Pearl Bailey began her career singing at clubs in New York City in the mid-1940s. She became best known for her renditions of "Bill Bailey, Won't You Please Come Home," "Tired," and "Toot Toot Tootsie Goodbye." Bailey's successful Broadway stage appearances in the 1940s and '50s led to a long film career with roles that showcased her musical, comic and dramatic talents. She is best known for her Tony Award-winning portrayal of Dolly Levi in an all-black version of *Hello, Dolly!*, which ran on Broadway in 1967. In 1971 she hosted her own television variety show, *The Pearl Bailey Show*, and later had a recurring role on the sitcom *Silver Spoons*. During her years in movies and television, Bailey remained active in politics and social concerns. She was named "Ambassador of Love" by President Nixon in 1968, and served as a special delegate to the United Nations under the Ford, Reagan, and Bush administrations. She died in 1990 in Philadelphia.

Pearl Bailey takes a curtain call in St. Louis Woman *in 1946.*

ELLA BAKER

Leading civil rights activist Ella Baker helped to found the Southern Christian Leadership Conference (SCLC) in the late 1950s, and later was instrumental in developing the Student Nonviolent Coordinating Committee (SNCC). She was born in 1903 in Norfolk, VA, to educated parents who worked hard to instill the value of learning and education in their children. During the 1940s, Baker began working for the NAACP, first as a field secretary, then as a director of branch offices. In the early 1950s, she moved to New York and began fund-raising activities for the civil rights struggles going on in the south. After some success, she moved back to Atlanta and joined the SCLC in 1958. During the 1960s, when students began leading sit-ins on college and university campuses, Baker left the SCLC to focus on developing the SNCC. She helped launch the Mississippi Freedom Democratic Party that challenged the all-white Democratic delegation at the 1964 presidential convention.

Baker's belief in the power of communal action had an enormous impact. During her career, she worked for all of the major civil rights organizations at their greatest time of need. Through her philosophy and actions, she motivated hundreds to act, to help themselves, and others. Ella Baker remained an activist until her death in 1986.

St. Louis-born Josephine Baker, shown in 1949, was a prime attraction in Paris.

JOSEPHINE BAKER

Born in St Louis, Missouri in 1906, Josephine Baker began her performing career as a chorus girl. Her first big break came at the age of 17, when she was chosen to perform in the musical comedy *Shuffle Along*, at Radio City Music Hall in 1923. The year 1925 was a turning point for Baker when she was spotted performing by an associate of the Théâtre des Champs-Elysées. She moved to Paris and from her first performance in *La Revue Nègre*, she was an overnight sensation. She left the show to create her most controversial role, that of "Dark Star" of the Folies Bérgère, in which she appeared topless on a mirror, with only a band of bananas around her waist.

The spectacular role made her a beloved star with a loyal following in France. In the 1930s she ventured into films and light opera. After serving with the Red Cross during World War II, she returned to the entertainment world, and made headlines in 1951 for speaking out against segregation and refusing to perform in segregated venues. In 1954 she began to earn a reputation as a progressive humanitarian, when she used her fortune to adopt and tutor a group of orphaned babies of different races. Baker retired from the stage in 1956 to devote herself full time to her "rainbow family." She returned to show business within a few years when the financial strain of raising a large, diverse family began to take its toll. Baker died in Paris in 1975, having performed earlier that same day in a gala celebrating her fiftieth year in show business.

JAMES BALDWIN

James Baldwin, born in Harlem in 1924, is a writer known for his honest perspective and often painful depiction of the effects of racism on both black and white Americans. His numerous novels, essays and plays reflect his experiences coming of age during the rise of the civil rights movement.

During the 1960s, many African-American writers criticized Baldwin for writing about homosexual experiences and for directing his work toward a white audience as well as a black one. He insisted that he was an "American writer," and that his work was a reflection of the multiracial and multicultural society he was a part of. Some of his most recognized novels are *Notes of a Native Son*, *Go Tell It On the Mountain*, *Tell Me How Long the Train's Been Gone*, and *If Beale Street Could Talk*. He won many awards during his lifetime, including an American Book Award nomination for the novel *Just Above My Head*, in 1979. Baldwin died of stomach cancer in 1987 at his home in St.-Paul-De-Vence, France.

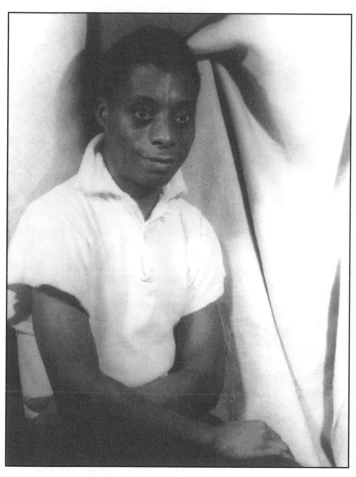

James Baldwin in 1955

IMAMU AMIRI BARAKA

Born LeRoi Jones in Newark, New Jersey in 1934, critically acclaimed playwright Amiri Baraka won fame as an Obie Award winning playwright for avant-garde theater. His reputation soared when his play, *Dutchman*, won the 1964 Obie for best play produced off-Broadway. Bakara wrote more than 20 plays, as well as 13 volumes of poetry, and essays on black culture, music and history. He founded the Black Arts Repertory Theater in Harlem, which became a major center for the development of black culture. Although he is a controversial figure due to his political beliefs—becoming a radical Black Nationalist in the 1960s, then a committed Marxist in the 70s—most critics agree that Bakara has had an enormous influence on black writing of the late twentieth century. His views have particularly affected the work of young black writers, and his plays have been produced in Paris, Berlin, Dakar and Senegal, as well as in the U.S.

COUNT BASIE

Born August 21, 1904, William "Count" Basie was one of the major Big Band and jazz orchestra leaders of the twentieth century, and is regarded as an important influence on jazz as a whole. He is best known for the formation of the Count Basie Orchestra, most prominent in the closing years of the 1930s swing era. The driving swing sound of the Basie orchestra was its trademark.

After performing vaudeville in Kansas City during the 1920s, Basie joined Walter Page's Blue Devils, playing a style of music known as the "Kansas City" sound. When Basie formed his own band in 1935, their style was heavily influenced by the Kansas City sound of his early days. Basie brought his group to New York in 1936, and within a year had cut his own record and was well on his way to becoming a force in the jazz world. In addition to making records during the 1950s, Basie's group toured Europe and became known as being used as a background orchestra for outstanding vocalists such as Frank Sinatra. The Basie Orchestra's hallmark was the rhythm section, which featured Basie's clean, spare piano style combined with the talent of bassist Walter Page and percussionist Jo Jones. Except for the years 1950–51, when he had a small group, Count Basie led a big band for almost forty years, until his death in 1984.

PEG LEG BATES

Born in South Carolina in 1907, Clayton (Peg Leg) Bates lost his left leg at the age of 12 in an accident at a cottonseed-gin mill where he worked. Undaunted, he was a self-taught dancer who overcame the handicap to acquire a career as a featured performer in vaudeville, Broadway musicals, and nightclub acts. Bates made more appearances on the *Ed Sullivan Show* than any other tap dancer. He died in December of 1998 in the same South Carolina town where he was born.

HARRY BELAFONTE

Harry Belafonte was born in New York City on March 1, 1927, and moved to Jamaica at the age of eight when rioting broke out in his Harlem neighborhood. After five years he returned to New York to attend high school, but clearly his time in Jamaica was embedded in his soul, as the sounds and songs he learned as a youngster became the vehicle to his greatest achievements as a performer.

In 1948 Belafonte joined the American Negro Theater (ANT), an influential group in Harlem during the 1940s. From there, he branched out into singing, performing popular songs and folk tunes at the Village Vanguard and other top clubs. His well known night club act led to opportunities on Broadway, where in 1953 Belafonte won a Tony award for his performance in *John Murray Anderson's Almanac*. A year later, when he starred with Dorothy Dandridge in *Carmen Jones*, his good looks and charm made him the nation's first black matinee idol.

Harry Belafonte learned music as a child in Jamaica.

Belafonte achieved his greatest fame as a singer in the 1950s, when he drew upon his early childhood in Jamaica and began performing West Indian calypso tunes. His 1956 album *Calypso*, which included Belafonte's unique rendition of such tunes as, "Matilda," "Shake Señora" and "Banana Boat Song" ("Day-O"), created a calypso craze in the United States and was the first solo album in history to sell more than a million copies. In following ten years Belafonte recorded 11 more albums while touring and giving concert performances. He became a close friend of Dr. Martin Luther King and was active in the civil right's movement, doing fundraising campaigns, participating in strategy sessions and attempting to educate government officials. Belafonte refused to perform in the South until segregation was abolished.

During the 1980s and 1990s, Harry Belafonte devoted himself to human rights causes throughout the world, aiding victims of famine in Africa, and serving as chairperson of the welcoming committee for Nelson Mandela's visit to the United States. In recognition of his efforts and contribution to the arts and society, he was appointed goodwill ambassador for UNICEF, and appointed the National Medal of Arts in 1994. In 1990, he was awarded an honorary doctorate from Spelman College.

CHUCK BERRY

Songwriter, singer and musician Chuck Berry's distinctive lyrical style and imaginative guitar playing has made him one of the true heroes of rock and roll music. His energetic ensemble sound facilitated the debut of bands from the Beach Boys to the Rolling Stones.

Born Charles Edward Anderson Berry in St. Louis on Oct. 18, 1926, he taught himself to play the guitar as a teenager. Playing in clubs and at parties, Berry formed a trio of musicians and experimented with writing his own songs and music for their performances. By 1955 the 28 year-old Berry had become a respected rhythm and blues guitarist and singer. He signed with Chess records, and made his way to superstardom with his hits "Roll Over Beethoven," "Rock and Roll Music," and the guitar anthem "Johnny B. Goode." Considering all the classic rock and roll tunes Berry had released over the years, it was surprising that his best selling single "My Ding-a-Ling," released in 1972, was his first number one hit on the *Billboard* pop charts. Berry has received numerous awards in his lifetime, including the American Music Conference's National Music Award, and a Grammy Award for Lifetime Achievement in 1984. He was inducted into the Rock and Roll Hall of Fame in 1986.

MARY McLEOD BETHUNE

Educator and civil rights leader Mary McLeod was born in 1875, the 15th of 17 children of parents who were former slaves emancipated after the Civil War. Determined to see their youngest surviving child educated, Mary's parents sent her to a mission school four or five miles from her rural home in South Carolina, and later to Scotia Seminary in North Carolina. At the age of twenty, she became a teacher and deciding to dedicate her life to the education of young children. She married Albertus Bethune in 1897.

Mary McCleod Bethune went on to create the Daytona Normal and Industrial School, later known as Bethune-Cookman College in Daytona, Florida. She became vice president of the National Urban League in 1920, served as president of the NAACP from 1924–1928, and established the National Council of Negro Women in 1935.

Working closely with Franklin D. Roosevelt's New Deal administration, Bethune served as director of the Division of Minority Affairs under the National Youth Administration from 1936 to 1943. In 1945, during World War II, she served as an assistant to the Secretary of War for the selection of candidates for the Women's Army Corps, as well as meeting her duties as a special representative of the State Department at the founding conference of the United Nations. She died in 1955.

EUBIE BLAKE

Born James Hubert Blake in Baltimore, Maryland on February 7, 1883, Eubie Blake was a prime innovator in African-American musical history. He composed such songs as "I'm Just Wild About Harry" and "Love Will Find a Way," which continue to be jazz and pop standards.

Blake began playing piano in 1899 and was active on the vaudeville circuit in his early years of performing. In 1915 he formed the Dixie Duo with Noble Sissle, and toured the world throughout World War I with James Europe. In 1921 the Duo created the music for *Shuffle Along*, a hugely popular show that ran on Broadway until 1928. Blake wrote and reviewed other popular shows, of note: *The Chocolate Dandies, Blackbirds of 1930* and *Swing It*. The huge success of *Shuffle Along* started a trend of Broadway shows featuring African-American performers. In the course of his musical career, he wrote more than three hundred songs, most of which were ragtime tunes. Eubie Blake's piano playing was a direct influence upon the Harlem stride piano style of Fats Waller and James P. Johnson.

Toward the end of his life, Blake received many honorary degrees, and in 1981 he won the Presidential Medal of Honor. His life was used as the basis for the 1978 Broadway show, *Eubie!*

JULIAN BOND

Controversial civil rights leader Julian Bond has had a long and diverse career in everything from politics to television. Along the way he has been labeled everything from national hero to national traitor. In the early 1960s, Bond helped create the Student Nonviolent Coordinating Committee (SNCC), and from 1974 to 1989, Bond served as president of the Atlanta branch of the NAACP. In 1975 he was elected to the Georgia Senate, where he remained until 1989. He has remains an influential voice in politics, education and the media. He has been a visiting professor at several universities, is a popular lecturer and writer, and has hosted the television show, *America's Black Forum*.

ARNA BONTEMPS

Born in 1902 in Alexandria, Virginia, Arna Bontemps was one of the key figures of the Harlem Renaissance, as well as one of the most prolific black writers of the twentieth century. He wrote more than 25 books, including fiction, poetry, criticism, history and biography. His memoirs and reminiscences of the Harlem Renaissance have been invaluable to historians, and his anthologies and introductions to the works of other black authors have helped define the study of black American literature. Bontemps wrote many books for young children, focusing on black history, culture and folklore. He died of a heart attack in 1973 in Nashville.

THOMAS BRADLEY

Thomas Bradley became the first African-American elected to the Los Angeles City Council in 1963, a position he served until 1971. In 1973 he became mayor and has been credited by some as turning the city into a modern metropolis. During Bradley's 20 years in office, Los Angeles developed into an important world city, adding a major international airport and hosting the 1984 summer Olympic games.

Bradley was born in Calvert, Texas, in 1917. His family later moved to Los Angeles, where he attended UCLA, and served 22 years in the police department. He earned his law degree from Southwestern University Law School in 1956.

Often considered one of the country's most powerful African-American politicians over the course of his twenty years as mayor of Los Angeles, Tom Bradley probably achieved the most notoriety toward the end of his career, during the 1992 riots. Challenged to heal the African-American community, he established several organizations and neighborhood programs designed to rebuild L.A. In 1993 he was honored for his years of service by the U.S. Conference of Mayors.

Bradley died in September, 1998, at the age of 80 after suffering a stroke that had left him partially paralyzed in 1996.

CAROL MOSLEY BRAUN

Carol Mosley Braun shocked political observers by scoring a stunning upset over incumbent Senator Alan Dixon in the Democratic Primary in Illinois on March 17, 1992. Her victory over the Republican candidate in November made her the first African-American woman to serve as U.S. Senator and the fourth African-American to serve in the Senate.

Braun was born in 1947 in Chicago. She graduated from the University of Illinois with a BA in political science, and went on to earn her law degree from the University of Chicago in 1972. After a successful campaign in 1977, she served in the Illinois State Legislature for 11 years. She then took a position as recorder of deeds for Cook County before deciding to run for the U.S. Senate in 1992.

GWENDOLYN BROOKS

Gwendolyn Brooks has been described as "one of the first American poets to use black speech in an artful way, and she has remained a master." Born in Topeka, Kansas in 1917, Brooks published her first book of poetry, *A Street in Bronzville*, in 1945. In the same year, she was named as one of *Mademoiselle* magazine's ten "Women of the Year." She was the first African-American to receive the Pulitzer Prize, in 1950 for her second book of poetry, *Annie Allen*. Brooks is a member of the National Academy of Arts and Letters, and was selected to be the first African-American woman poetry consultant to the Library of Congress. She has always emphasized that that her writing might be "to blacks," but that it was "for anyone who wants to open the book." Brooks's work has been collected in *Selected Poems*, published in 1963, *The World of Gwendolyn Brooks* (1971), and *Blacks* (1987). She has written two writing manuals for young poets, and contributes money to sponsor national poetry contests for young people. In 1994 Brooks was honored by the National Book Foundation for distinguished contributions to American Letters.

JAMES BROWN

Though he often claims to have been born in 1933 in Macon, Georgia, James Brown was actually born May 3, 1928 in Barnwell, South Carolina. Dubbed "The Hardest Working Man in Show Business," "The Godfather of Soul," and the "Minister of the New New Super Heavy Funk," Brown is one of the most dynamic performers of the century and has been a strong influence on most forms of black music—soul, hip-hop, funk and R&B. A highlight of Brown's early career was the release of *Live At The Apollo* in

James Brown, "The Godfather of Soul," in 1991

1963. This was followed by the hits "Papa's Got A Brand New Bag" and "I Got You (I Feel Good)" in 1965. Brown continues to perform today.

JIM BROWN

Considered by many to be the best football player of all time, Jim Brown led the National Football League in rushing for eight of his nine years, and held the career mark for nineteen years after his retirement in 1965.

Born February 17, 1936, Brown grew up in Manhasset, Long Island where he lived with his grandmother. By the time he finished high school he had earned varsity letters in baseball, football, basketball, track and lacrosse. Following graduation Brown had a choice of 42 college scholarships, as well as professional offers from both the New York Yankees and the Boston Braves. He chose Syracuse University, where he became an All-American in both football and lacrosse. Upon graduating from college, Brown was drafted to the NFL by Cleveland, and became an immediate star. Not only did he lead the league in rushing, he brought the team to a division championship, and was unanimously named Rookie of the Year. His best season came in 1963, when he rushed for 1,863 yards and was named the NFL's

Player of the Year. In 1964 he led the Browns to an NFL championship.

When Brown announced his retirement in 1966, he was only thirty years old. He went on to pursue an acting career and made several films, including *Rio Conchos*, *The Dirty Dozen*, and *100 Rifles*. His experiences as an African-American athlete are recounted in his 1964 autobiography, *Off My Chest*.

RONALD H. BROWN

Ronald H. Brown was born in 1941, grew up in Harlem, New York, where he attended private schools, and went on to Middlebury College, where he was instrumental in integrating the fraternity system. He graduated in 1962 with a degree in political science. After serving in the Armed Forces in West Germany and Korea, he went on to earn a law degree from St. John's University. In 1973, Brown moved to Washington where he eventually became the second ranking figure in the Urban League's national office. He continued with them until 1979, working over the years as general counsel, Washington spokesperson, deputy executive director, and vice-president of Washington operations. In 1979 he joined Senator Edward Kennedy's presidential campaign as deputy manager. He was appointed to the Senate Judicial Committee in 1980 by Kennedy. During the 1980s Brown continued his legal work and became a partner in a Washington law firm. In 1989 he was elected chairman of the Democratic National Committee, making him the first African-American to head a major political party. In 1993, President Clinton appointed Brown to serve on his cabinet as Secretary of Commerce. Ron Brown died in a plane crash on April 3, 1996, near the Croatian coast while on a commerce mission in the war-torn Balkans.

GRACE BUMBRY

Grace Ann Bumbry made her operatic debut in 1960 with the Paris Opera Company in *Aida*, and was the first black performer to sing at the Wagner Festival in Bayreuth, Germany in 1961. Bumbry has been a mainstay at New York's Metropolitan Opera since her debut, and is one of the few singers who has been called to play a command performance at the White House. She is the recipient of many awards, including a Grammy in 1979.

RALPH JOHNSON BUNCHE

Ralph Bunche was the first African-American to win the Nobel Peace Prize, awarded to him in 1950 for his successful intervention in the Arab-Israeli conflict at the time of the founding of Israel.

One of many "black heroes" who rose to prominence in the 1950s and 1960s, *Newsweek* magazine called Bunche, "the foremost negro of his generation—the distinguished symbol of how far a black man could rise in the Establishment." Admired far and wide, he considered his own greatest accomplishment to be his work on the Suez area of Egypt, where between 1956 and 1957 he organized and directed 6,000 UN peace keeping troops. He was appointed undersecretary to the United Nations in 1955, the highest rank achieved by a black American, and served at the UN until his death in 1971.

Ralph Bunche in 1951.

CAB CALLOWAY

Band leader Cab Calloway, a pioneer of scat singing (improvisational rhythmic syllable), was known for his signature phrase, "Hi-de-ho" from his theme song "Minnie the Moocher" (1931).

Born Cabell Calloway in Rochester, New York, in 1907, he grew up in Baltimore and began singing with his church choir as a child. Calloway performed at New York's famous Cotton Club and made his Broadway debut in *Blackbirds of 1928*, singing "I Can't Give You Anything But Love." His first band, the Alabamians, was formed in 1929, and became Cab Calloway and His Orchestra, the highest paid of the black bands in the 1930s and 1940s. Many notable jazz musicians of the day played in Calloway's band at one time or another, including trumpeter Dizzy Gillespie, and saxophonists Ben Webster and Chu Berry.

Calloway appeared in many films during the 1930s and 1940s as well, including *The Big Broadcast* (1932), *Manhattan Merry-Go-Round* (1937), and *Stormy Weather* (1943). He starred on Broadway in the musical *The Pajama Game* and the all-black version of *Hello Dolly!* A flamboyant figure especially known for his style, Calloway is said to have invented the baggy zoot suit. He was the model for the character Sportin' Life in the Geshwin opera *Porgy and Bess*, a role he played himself in the 1950s. Calloway was featured in the 1980 film *The Blues Brothers*. He was presented the National Medal of the Arts by President Clinton. Calloway died in Delaware in 1994.

ROY CAMPANELLA

The first African-American catcher in major league baseball history, Roy Campanella was voted Most Valuable Player in the National League three times during his nine full seasons with the Brooklyn Dodgers.

Campanella was born November 19, 1915 in Philadelphia. He joined the Negro League's Baltimore Elite Giants right out of high school, and quickly became a star player, named to All-Star teams in 1941, 1944, and 1945.

The following season, Campanella became the second black player to sign with Brooklyn (the first was Jackie Robinson), and by 1949 he became the Dodgers' regular catcher. Known for his outstanding ability to handle pitchers, "Campy" caught three no-hitters, led the league in putouts six times, caught 100 or more games a year his last nine years in the majors, and nailed two of every three runners who tried to steal on him. He played in five World Series games, hitting two home runs in the Dodgers' only World Series win in 1953. His career total was 242 homers.

Roy Campanella won National League Most Valuable Player awards in 1951, 1953, and 1955.

In 1958, Campanella's career was cut short when the car he was driving struck a utility pole, leaving him paralyzed. His personal account of the tragedy was published in his book, *It's Good to Be Alive*, in 1959. In May of the same year, baseball's all-time record crowd of 93,103 filled the Los Angeles Coliseum to pay tribute to the heroic catcher. Ten years later, Campanella became the second African-American player—after Robinson—to be elected to the Baseball Hall of Fame.

WILLIAM WARRICK CARDOZO

Pioneering doctor, W. Warrick Cardozo was born in 1905 in Washington, D.C. While studying medicine he received a research grant to study sickle cell anemia, now known as sickle cell disease. It was his work that discovered that sickle cell disease is an inherited condition, found almost exclusively in people of African descent. Dr. Cardozo died of a heart attack in 1962.

STOKELY CARMICHAEL

Born in 1941 on the Caribbean island of Trinidad/Tobago, Stokely Carmichael ascended to fame in the 1960s, as one of the most powerful and influential leaders of the Student Non-Violent Coordinating Committee (SNCC). Best known for popularizing the dynamic phrase, "Black Power," he became a controversial figure in the 1960s due to his association with the Black Panther party. After traveling throughout the world to escape scrutiny by the FBI in the US, he changed his name in 1978 to Kwame Toure, in honor of the two men who most influenced the Pan-African philosophical education he had taken up in Guinea. Toure continues to travel throughout the world, working toward a united African people.

BETTY CARTER

Known as the "Godmother of Jazz," for helping and mentoring new performers, Betty Carter created her own musical identity through her singing, composing and arranging.

Born Lille Mae Jones in 1929, Carter studied at the Detroit Conservatory of Music, and began singing with such musical greats as Dizzy Gillespie, Charlie Parker, Miles Davis and Lionel Hampton while still in her teens. In 1969 she started her own record label, Bet-Car Productions. Perhaps her best-known tune, "Baby It's Cold Outside," was a duet recorded with Ray Charles. She made more than 15 albums during her career, and in 1988 won a Grammy award for Best Female Jazz Vocalist. President Clinton presented Carter with the National Medal of the Arts in 1997. She died on September 28, 1998, of pancreatic cancer.

GEORGE WASHINGTON CARVER

Although George Washington Carver is best known in history books as the man who invented new uses for the peanut, an accomplishment of greater impact was actually his saving southern agriculture from an excessive dependence on cotton.

Born a slave in 1864 in Missouri, Carver was separated from his mother at an early age and sold by his master for a race horse. He managed to get a high school education while working on a farm, and was the first black student admitted to Simpson College in Iowa. From there he earned a master's degree at Iowa Agricultural College (now Iowa State U.), and became the first African-American to serve on its faculty. In 1896, Booker T. Washington offered him a post at the Tuskegee Institute in Alabama.

While there, Carver transformed the southern agricultural economy by showing that 300 products could be derived from the peanut. By 1938, peanuts had become a $200 million industry. He also created over 100 products from the sweet potato, 500 dyes from various southern plants, synthetic marble made from sawdust, woven rugs made from okra stalks; and wallboards from pinecones, peanut shells and banana stems. Although he did hold three patents, Carver never pursued patenting his inventions, saying, "God gave them to me, how can I sell them?"

Carver died in 1943, and was buried next to Booker T. Washington at the Tuskegee Institute. In 1953, Congress erected a George Washington Carver National Monument in Missouri—the first federal monument dedicated to an African-American.

WILT CHAMBERLAIN

Born in 1936 in Philadelphia, Pennsylvania, Wilton Norman Chamberlain—Wilt "the Stilt"—grew to be seven feet tall and became one the greatest offensive players in the history of basketball. During his high school years he already dominated the courts, once scoring 90 points in a 36-minute game. He holds the current NBA record for most points in one game, an amazing 100.

In 1956, while attending the University of Kansas, Chamberlain led his team to a record of 24 wins and 3 losses his first year on varsity. He was an All-American in 1957 and 1958 and led his team to the 1958 NCAA finals. His impact on college basketball was enormous. To keep Chamberlain from standing under the basket and dominating the action in games, college officials changed some of the rules: outlawing offensive goal-tending and widening the foul lane, among others.

Growing tired of the efforts to hold him back in college basketball, he left school after his junior year and toured briefly with the Harlem Globetrotters. The NBA's Philadelphia Warriors had already drafted Chamberlain, but he was unable to join the team until 1959 when his college class graduated, due to league rules. In his first season with the Warriors he became the first rookie player

ever to be chosen both Rookie of the Year and Most Valuable Player. Over the course of his 14 seasons in professional basketball—with the Philadelphia Warriors, the San Francisco Warriors, the Philadelphia 76ers and the Los Angeles Lakers—Chamberlain led the NBA in scoring 7 times and won 11 rebounding titles. When he retired after the 1973 season, he had scored a record 31,419 points, the first player in the game to score over 30,000. In 1978 Chamberlain was elected to the Basketball Hall of Fame.

Wilt Chamberlain was elected to the Basketball Hall of Fame in 1978.

RAY CHARLES

Singer-keyboardist Ray Charles has been credited as one of the founders of soul music.

Growing up in Florida, Charles developed an eye disease that left him completely blind by the age of seven. He received his first musical training while attending a school for the blind, and subsequently left school at the age of 15 to play in local musical engagements.

In 1957, Charles released his first album, consisting of a mix of instrumentals drawn from popular music, gospel, and modern jazz. His unique blend of blues and gospel spirit

The great singer Ray Charles performing in Paris in May, 1983.

Care division of New York City's Bureau of Child Welfare.

In 1964, Chisolm was elected New York State Assemblywoman representing the 55th district in New York City. In 1968 she was elected to the U.S. House of Representatives, a position she served in until her retirement in 1982. Chisolm served on the Democratic National Committee, was a delegate to the Democratic National Mid-Term Conference in 1974, and was a candidate for the 1972 Democratic presidential nomination.

Chisolm retired from politics in 1982. Despite her departure from elective office, she remains a spokesperson for the oppressed, and has always been a strong advocate for women. Chisolm is a member of the NAACP, the National Association of Colored Women, and the League of Women Voters.

was the beginning of the sound known as "soul" music, and "brother Ray" became a cultural icon in the subsequent decades. One of the world's most popular performers, Charles even had a stint as spokesperson for Pepsi in the 1980s–early 1990s. The recipient of more than 10 Grammy awards, he was awarded the National Medal of Arts in 1993, and is enrolled in the Rock and Roll Hall of Fame. Charles is also an inductee of the Playboy Jazz and Pop Hall of Fame and the Songwriters Hall of Fame.

SHIRLEY CHISOLM

A model of independence and integrity, Shirley Chisolm has made extensive contributions to society in politics, education and feminism. During her nearly forty year career she faced constant obstacles not only as an African American, but also as a woman. She has always been an advocate of women's issues, and has been noted for making the observation that it is often more difficult to be a woman than to be black.

Born in 1924 in Brooklyn, New York, Chisolm graduated cum laude from Brooklyn College in 1946. After an early career in preschool and childhood education, which culminated in her directorship of the Hamilton-Madison Child Care Center in New York, she served as a consultant to the Day

Prominent educator, politician and feminist Shirley Chisolm.

BILL COSBY

One of the nation's richest and most popular entertainers, Bill Cosby's early career success was a breakthrough for African-Americans and he has continuously pressed the frontier in television and comedy.

Born in 1937 in Germantown, Pennsylvania, Cosby was the oldest of William Cosby senior and Annie Perle Cosby's four sons. The family was poor and lived in a low-income, all black housing project. Although he had a high IQ, his intelligence did not transfer into good grades, and Cosby ended up dropping out of high school and joining the Navy. While serving, he completed his high school education through a correspondence course, and upon his discharge, he enrolled in Temple University with a football scholarship.

Cosby began performing stand up routines at local clubs to help support himself during college, and soon became known around Philadelphia. In 1962, left school and took his stand up comedy routine to New York, where he performed at the Gaslight Café in Greenwich Village on weekends.

After marrying Camille Hanks in 1964, Cosby's career took off, and he began traveling around the country performing in popular clubs and nightspots. His big break came in 1965 when he appeared on the *Tonight Show with Johnny Carson*. His performance impressed the television producer Sheldon Leonard, and he was cast as a secret agent in the TV adventure series *I Spy*. Cosby broke television's color barrier by becoming the first black star in a television series that excluded racial themes. The show ran for three seasons, earning Cosby two successive Emmy Awards.

Bill Cosby, shown here in 1998.

His first sitcom, *The Bill Cosby Show*, aired from 1969 to 1971. He also hosted and produced the cartoon series *Fat Albert and the Cosby Kids*, made regular appearances on various children's programs, appeared in movies, and at the same time recorded a string of Grammy Award winning comedy albums. During these years Cosby resumed his education, earning a B.A from Temple University and a doctorate in education from University of Massachusetts. The Cosbys' concern for education has led them to provide generous financial support to educational institutions over the years, most notably a $20 million donation to Spelman College in Atlanta.

In 1984, Cosby's career reached new heights with the television series *The Cosby Show*. The show remained on the air through 1991, ranking as television's number one show. Cosby has also become a best selling author, with his successful series of books (*Fatherhood, Childhood, Love and Marriage*, and others) humorously reflecting his struggles with parenthood.

Fate dealt Cosby a cruel blow in 1997 when his son, Ennis, was shot to death during an attempted holdup in Los Angeles. Despite his grief, Cosby has continued working, returning to stand up comedy and launching another new television series in 1998.

JOHN HENRIK CLARKE

Internationally renowned historian and writer John Henrik Clarke was one of nine children born to a sharecropper in 1915. He became interested in stories about black people and ancient history as a result of his Bible studies growing up in Georgia.

Clarke arrived in New York in 1933, just at the end of the Harlem Renaissance. He studied at New York University and the New School for Social Research, concentrating in history and world literature. In addition to being an author and editor of more than twenty books, he was co-founder of the *Harlem Quarterly* in 1949. He was also a founding member of the Harlem Writer's Guild. In addition to his writing and journalism career, Clarke has taught in many community-based institutions, and began serving as professor of African World History at Hunter College in New York City in 1967. In 1969 Clarke was chosen as the first president of the African Heritage Studies Association (AHSA). He retired from teaching in 1988, and since then has served Hunter College as professor emeritus of the department of Africana and Puerto Rican studies.

ELDRIDGE CLEAVER

Eldridge Cleaver was born in Arkansas in 1935, and grew up in the Watts district of Los Angeles. By the time he was a teen he started running into trouble, and was arrested for various thefts and drug deals. Spending most of his later teens and twenties in and out of prison, Cleaver completed his high school education while incarcerated. Away from the temptations of the outside world, he went on to study political science, and also joined the Black Muslims, a sect advocating black separatism from white society. In the late 50s and early 60s, he was particularly inspired by Malcolm X, a prominent Black Muslim, and followed his lead when he broke from the party.

During his time in prison, Cleaver was able to smuggle out some of his writings about his life, and in 1966, the magazine *Ramparts* published a few of his essays. Later that year, through the efforts of the editors at *Ramparts* and noted literary figures such as Norman Mailer, Cleaver received parole. Upon release he joined the Black Panther party. Clashes between Black Panthers and the police occurred in Oakland, California, where Cleaver was an editor at *Ramparts*. After one particularly violent conflict, which resulted in the death of a Black Panther member and the wounding of a police officer, Cleaver was again arrested and ordered back to prison. Cleaver instead chose to flee and became a fugitive from justice. After several years wandering abroad, Cleaver converted to Christianity, returned to the United States and surrendered to federal authorities. This time he received a much lighter sentence of 2,000 hours of community service.

The 1978 publication of Cleaver's autobiography, *Soul on Ice*—a collection of essays on black rage and alienation, interracial relationships and life inside prison walls—catapulted him to fame and became a manifesto for much of the black power movement. But toward the end of his life, he angered and mystified many of his former allies by becoming a conservative Republican. He died on May 1, 1998.

NAT KING COLE

Born Nathaniel Coles in Montgomery, Alabama in 1919, by the time he was 12 Nat was playing organ and singing in church with his three brothers, all of whom also became jazz musicians. After making his record debut with his brother Eddie Cole's Solid Swingers in 1936, Coles formed the King Cole Trio (minus the final 's') in California in 1938. Rumor has it that the title "King" was given to him

King Cole Trio at Savoy Ballroom, Kansas City, Missouri

when the trio appeared in Hollywood and the manager urged him to wear a gold paper crown on his head.

As the trio gained popularity during the early 1940s, Cole made the full transition from jazz pianist to pop singer. By 1947 his fame reached phenomenal levels, his records selling millions of copies. Maria Cole's (Nat's second wife and the mother of his children) 1971 biography, *Nat King Cole*, lists over 800 titles released between November 1943 and March 1965, including some of his best known: "Mona Lisa," "Unforgettable," "Embraceable You," "Chestnuts Roasting on an Open Fire" and "When I Fall in Love."

Cole appeared successfully in several film musicals during his career. His final film was *Cat Ballou*, completed just prior to his death. He died of lung cancer in February of 1965, at the age of 45.

JOHN COLTRANE

John Coltrane was a great innovator who strongly influenced the course of jazz music. Born September 23, 1926 in Hamlet, North Carolina, he played saxophone in the Navy band before joining Dizzy Gillespie's big band in 1949. After the band broke up, he played tenor sax with Earl Bostic and Johnny Hodges until he was hired by Miles Davis in 1955. The most productive part of Coltrane's career was between the years 1955 and 1967, during which time his highly individual style reshaped modern jazz and came to influence generations of other musicians. He formed his own quartet, which became one of the most tightly knit groups in jazz history. In 1960 the quartet recorded Coltrane's biggest hit, *My Favorite Things*, in a marathon session that featured his soprano sax and lasted more than fifteen minutes. He died in 1967 from liver cancer, at the age of 41.

SAM COOKE

Singer-songwriter Sam Cooke was the first African American gospel star to achieve success in popular music with his hit song, "You Send Me," which reached number one on the pop charts in 1957 and sold almost two million copies.

Cooke was born in Mississippi in 1931, but his family moved to Chicago shortly after he was born. Already a popular singer with gospel groups as a teenager, in 1950 he was offered a spot in one of the top American Gospel groups, The Soul Stirrers.

Cooke's move from gospel music into pop and R & D was not popular with the gospel music circuit, but his success in 1957 launched a major solo career. His hits included "Chain Gang," "Twisting the Night Away," "Shake," and others. Cooke died suddenly in 1994, shot by a hotel manager in a seedy part of Los Angeles.

COUNTEE CULLEN

Born in 1903, Countee Cullen, a major writer of the Harlem Renaissance in the 1920s, was best known for writing about Africa and its meaning to black Americans. A graduate of New York University with a masters degree from Harvard, his first book of poetry, Color, was published in 1925, followed two years later by *Copper Sun* and *The Ballad of the Girl*. He was the author of of the novel, *One Way To Heaven* (1932) and with Arna Bontemps, co-authored a musical play, *St. Louis Woman*. Among his best known poems is "Yet Do I Marvel."

Although he was praised for his writing about black life and for his racial themes, Cullen insisted that he was a poet, not a "negro poet." In spite of this, he wrote poetry that focused on the difference between the hardships in racist America, and the beauty of his ancestral land. He was a mentor to James Baldwin, whom he met while teaching at Frederick Douglas High school in New York.

Cullen was married to W.E.B. Dubois' daughter, Nina. The 1928 wedding was considered a major social event during the Harlem Renaissance. They divorced two years later. Cullen died in 1946 at the age of 42.

ANGELA DAVIS

Political activist Angela Davis is co-founder and leader of the National Alliance Against Racist and Political Repression.

Davis was born in 1944 and grew up in Alabama during the time when segregation was in full force. While earning her M.A. in the late 1960s from the University of San Diego, Davis helped to found the Black Student Council and the Student Nonviolent Coordinating Committee, a major civil rights organization of the time. In 1969, she began her teaching career as a professor of philosophy at UCLA, but was dismissed because of her radical, communist political views. The American Association of University Professors protested her dismissal, and although a court ordered her reinstated, her subsequent contract was not renewed.

In 1970 Davis was accused of helping to plan the escape from prison of black activist George Jackson and supplying a gun that killed four people. She was sent to prison for 16 months, until she was acquitted of the charges and freed. She has since continued working on behalf of other political prisoners, traveling the world speaking on political topics. Davis is currently a professor at University of Santa Cruz, California, where she teaches African-American and feminist studies, and is on the board of directors of the National Political Congress of Black Women and of the National Black Women's Health Project.

MILES DAVIS

Musician and composer Miles Davis was a major influence in the transition from bebop, to the softer, more subtle "cool" jazz.

Born in Santa Monica, California in 1926, Davis played trumpet semiprofessionally as a teenager St. Louis jazz bands in the 1940s. In 1945 he was sent to the Julliard School in New York, and within a short time was working the 52nd Street jazz clubs with Charlie Parker and Coleman Hawkins. He formed his own nine-piece band in 1949,

which although short-lived, had a great impact on musicians and defined "cool" jazz.

During the 1950s and 1960s, Davis was adept at discovering new talent, including saxophonists John Coltrane, Cannonball Adderly, and Wayne Shorter, pianist Herbie Hancock, bassists Ron Carter and Paul Chambers, and drummers Philly Joe Jones and Tony Williams. His enthusiasm and encouragement of these jazz musicians made him an influential leader of jazz. Davis continued as a major force in the 1970s, gradually leaving pure jazz and using jazz fusion as a move toward contemporary black pop music. Miles Davis died in 1991 in Santa Monica.

OSSIE DAVIS

Actor, director and writer Ossie Davis was born in 1917 in Georgia, and grew up in the south. He attended Howard University and Columbia University before World War II. During the war he spent three years in the army where he wrote and produced shows for the troops. He met his wife, actess Ruby Dee, while they were performing together in the Broadway production of *Jeb Turner* in 1946. They formed a team at home and work, starring together on stage and in films during the 1950s and 60s.

A critically acclaimed playwright, Davis's adaptation of his own work *Purlie Victorious*, first to film and then to a Broadway musical in 1970 was praised by the *New York Times* as "by far the most successful and richest of all black musicals." His directing and producing brought him further success in 1970, with the film *Cotton Comes to Harlem*. He continued to act, produce and direct in films and television throughout the 1970s and 1980s. Ossie Davis always brought a political perspective and underlying message to his work, and has devoted himself to numerous causes, particularly those involving civil rights.

SAMMY DAVIS, Jr.

Sammy Davis, Jr., often called the world's greatest entertainer, earned the title with his remarkable versatility as a singer, actor, dancer, mimic and musician.

Davis was born in New York City on December 8, 1925, to parents who were both dancers at the peak of their careers. By the age of four he was appearing with his father in a vaudeville act known as the Will Mastin Trio. When he

Sammy Davis, Jr. appearing at Grosvenor House in London in July 1974.

Davis had performing roles on Broadway in *Golden Boy* and the jazz drama *A Man Called Adam*. His 1966 autobiography, *Yes I Can*, was a bestseller, and he starred in his own network television series, "The Sammy Davis Show" and "Sammy & Company." His signature songs included "Mr. Bojangles," "What Kind of Fool Am I?" and "I've Gotta Be Me," and in 1972 he hit the top of the charts with "Candy Man." His movie credits over the years included *The Benny Goodman Story*, *Porgy & Bess*, and *Robin and the Seven Hoods*.

In 1968, the NAACP awarded Davis its Spingarn Medal for his outstanding achievements. He was married three times and had three children by his second wife. Sammy Davis, Jr. died in 1990 of throat cancer. Before he died, he made the film *Tap* in 1989, with Gregory Hines; a tribute to all the "hoofers" who had entertained so many for so long.

RUBY DEE

Perhaps best known for her performance in the film version of *Raisin in the Sun*, actress Ruby Dee's career

Ruby Dee in 1962.

entered the Army in 1943, he spent his two years of service writing, directing and producing camp shows. After his discharge he made his way to Hollywood, breaking into the "big time" with successful nightclub engagements.

During the late 1940s Davis toured and performed with other rising stars, including Mickey Rooney, Bob Hope, Frank Sinatra, Jack Benny and Eddie Cantor. He signed with Decca records in 1954, the same year that he lost an eye in a car accident. He was in great demand once he could perform again, with popular singles such as "Something's Gotta Give" and "That Old Black Magic." Davis scored a hit when he opened in his first Broadway show, *Mr. Wonderful*, in 1956. By the end of the 1950s, Davis was appearing regularly on television in variety shows such as Ed Sullivan.

In the 1960s Davis became a member of Hollywood's notorious "Rat Pack," led by Frank Sinatra and including Dean Martin, Peter Lawford, Joey Bishop, Tony Curtis and Henry Silva. The "Pack" starred in films together, such as *Oceans Eleven*, and became known as a group of inseparable fast-living, heavy-smoking, hard-drinking party boys.

WILLIAM E. B. DUBOIS

Writer and scholar William DuBois helped found the National Association for the Advancement of Colored People (NAACP), which for many years has been the major civil rights organization in the United States.

He was born William Edward Burghardt DuBois in 1868 in Great Barrington, Massachusetts. Though his family was poor, he enrolled in Fisk University upon graduating from high school. From there he transferred to Harvard University, where he graduated cum laude. In 1895, DuBois was the first African-American to earn a Ph.D. from Harvard. He became a professor of history and economics, and wrote many key works, including *The Souls of Black Folks*, in the years following.

A strong advocate for higher education for blacks, Dubois founded the Niagra Movement in 1905. The organization was a precursor to the NAACP, which was founded by black and white leaders in 1909. In 1910, Dubois left academia to become the NAACP's only black officer. Until 1934, he was editor of the association's journal, *Crisis*, where he was able to expound on his theory that black intelligentsia's leadership could elevate the social position of blacks as a whole.

In the 1940's Dubois participated in the organization of the United Nations, and remained active in the Pan-African movement, as well as left-wing American politics. In 1948 he was fired from the NAACP for his outspoken views on foreign policy. The government indicted him for being a Soviet agent in 1951, and although he was found innocent, he continued to be hassled with right-wing persecution. Regardless,

A strong advocate for higher education for African Americans, Wiliam Dubois helped found the NAACP. This portrait was taken in July, 1946.

DuBois remained supportive of the Soviet Union, which he saw as being a strong advocate of African independence.

He joined the Communist Party of the United States in 1961, and later that year was invited by the left-wing president of Ghana to live in his country. William DuBois became a citizen of Ghana, where he died in 1963—on the eve of the historical civil rights march on Washington. In an about-face of the federal government's long-term attitude toward DuBois, in 1976 his birthplace was designated a historical landmark.

began at the American Negro Theater (ANT) in Harlem, in 1941.

Dee was born in 1923 in Cleveland, Ohio as Ruby Ann Wallace. She began studying at the ANT while attending Hunter College in New York City. It was there, in 1943, that she met her future husband, Ossie Davis. Together they have performed in numerous films, plays and television shows, including co-hosting the PBS series *With Ossie and Ruby*. In 1965, Dee broke theatrical ground at the American Shakespeare Festival in Stratford, Connecticut as the first black actress to play major classical roles. As a writer she collaborated on the screenplay for the film *Up Tight*, in 1968, and by herself wrote, directed, and starred in the stage musical, *Take It From the Top*. She is also an accomplished poet, with three published collections, and was once a columnist for New York's major black newspaper, the *New York Amsterdam News*. Dee's one-woman show, *My One Good Nerve*, based on her book of the same title, premiered in New York in 1998.

FATS DOMINO

Pianist and singer Fats Domino was one of the first "crossover" artists who helped to develop and establish the New Orleans rhythm and blues sound, and to define the range of rock and roll piano.

Born Antoine Domino in New Orleans in 1928, he was self-taught on piano, and began playing in local clubs in the early 1940s. Domino formed his own group in 1950 and recorded with Imperial Records during the 50s and early 60s. During this time he became an influential figure in the growth of rhythm and blues and the emergence of rock and roll. By appearing in popular teen films in the 1950s, he gained popularity with both white and African American listeners. Domino recorded an enormous number of classic rock and roll hits, including "Ain't That a Shame," "I'm Walkin'," "Blue Monday," and "Blueberry Hill." One of the founders of rock and roll, more than sixty-five million of his records have been sold.

PAUL LAURENCE DUNBAR

One of the first African-American poets to gain national recognition, Paul Laurence Dunbar was known for his talent in using both black dialect and standard English in his writing. Born in Ohio in 1872, he was the most popular African-American writer in America at the turn of the twentieth century.

As a boy, Dunbar was seen as a black prodigy in a white world; he excelled in school, but was forced to take a job as an elevator operator upon graduating. He continued to write poetry while working, and published his first collection, *Oak and Ivy*, in 1893. Another volume followed, and in 1896, with the publication of *Lyrics of a Lowly Life*, his reputation was established. His subsequent works included six volumes of poetry, four novels, and four volumes of short stories. At the time of his death from tuberculosis in 1906, he was considered by the American public to be the dean of black poets. Dunbar's collection, *Completed Poems*, was published after his untimely death at the age of 33. The book has enjoyed such popularity that to this day it has never gone out of print.

Fats Domino came from New Orleans to fill the London's Olympia Theater with jazz, blues, and rock and roll.

KATHERINE DUNHAM

Dancer Katherine Dunham is an internationally known choreographer, teacher and anthropologist who introduced and popularized Afro-Caribbean dance throughout the world.

Dunham was born in 1909 in Chicago, and grew up in the white suburb of Glen Ellen. While attending the University of Chicago, she chose to do her fieldwork in the Caribbean, where she could study African-based ritual dancing, as well as the role of dance in popular culture. She received a Guggenheim Award in 1937 to continue her investigation of Caribbean dance. To complete her Ph.D.,

Katherine Dunham in May, 1940.

LEE ELDER

Professional golfer Lee Elder was the first African-American to play in a Masters tournament; the first African-American to break the $100,000 mark in yearly earnings; and the first African-American member of the U.S. Ryder Cup team.

Born in 1934, Elder grew up in Dallas, Texas and got his first exposure to golf working as a caddy. After winning the title in the African-American United Golfer's Association tournament in 1950, Elder turned professional. He joined the PGA in 1967, and in 1968 finished second to Jack Nicklaus in a dramatic "sudden death" play-off at the American Golf Classic in Akron, Ohio. In his first full year as a rookie on the PGA tour, Elder finished in the top sixty winners in the United States. He is one of a select group of PGA tour players to win three consecutive events, and became one of the top fifty all-time money winners. In 1971, Elder was the first black player in the South African PGA Open. In 1974, he founded the Lee Elder Scholarship Fund to provide financial aid to worthy college students.

Dunham wrote a thesis, "Dances of Haiti," which was later published in Spanish, French and English. In 1943, the Katherine Dunham School of Arts and Research opened in New York.

Based on her research in both Afro-Caribbean dance and cultural anthropology, Dunham introduced a new dance technique called "dance-isolation," which involves movement of one part of the body while the other parts are kept stationary. An important part of Dunham's aesthetic is self-mastery and empowerment. Of herself, she has said, "I am not a dancer, I am not an ethnologist. I am an evangelist."

Since her last performance in 1965, at the Apollo Theater in Harlem, Dunham has been the director of the Performing Arts Training Center, which she founded in St. Louis. In 1966, she served as cultural adviser to the president of Senegal. Her involvement in international affairs continued into the 1990s.

DUKE ELLINGTON

The "Duke" was born Edward Kennedy Ellington in 1899 in Washington, D.C., and began piano lessons at the age of six. He formed his first group in 1919, and moved to New York to try to break into its competitive music scene. His group, the Washingtonians, performed in a Times Square club and made the music tour of New England in the summers.

Ellington's big break came when they performed at Harlem's famous Cotton Club. His orchestra grew, recorded their first songs, appeared in Broadway musicals and films, and toured Europe on and off during the later 1920s and 1930s. He earned the nickname "Duke" because of his elegant way of dressing.

Duke Ellington, the "King of Swing."

RALPH ELLISON

Writer Ralph Ellison's best known work, the 1952 novel *Invisible Man*, won the National Book Award and in a 1965 literary poll was deemed "the most distinguished single work" published in the United States since 1945.

Ellison was born in 1914 in Oklahoma City. After attending the Tuskegee Institute in Alabama, he moved to New York in 1936. From 1938 to 1942, Ellison worked with the Federal Writer's Project, a federally-funded program designed to combat unemployment while supporting the arts. He published poems and short stories in left-wing journals, and in 1942, briefly edited the *Negro Quarterly*.

After serving in World War II, he received a grant from the Julius Rosenwald Fund that afforded him the time to begin working on *Invisible Man*, which took him seven years to write. The book, a story of one black man's journey from innocence to knowledge, and won numerous awards and much acclaim. The success of *Invisible Man* led to lecture tours and teaching positions at Yale and University of Chicago. Ralph Ellison died in 1994.

In 1995 a collection of short stories, *Flying Home and Other Stories*, was published; it included some of the best of the published stories, as well as unpublished stories discovered by the literary executor of Ellison's estate. With the help of Ellison's widow, Fanny, an unpublished novel, *Juneteenth*, begun in the 1940s and still being expanded at the time of his death—a novel that Ellison envisioned as a majestic story and perhaps a multi-volume cycle—was edited by his executor and published in 1999.

JULIUS ERVING

Julius Erving, also known as "Dr. J," was one of the leading career scorers in pro basketball. In sixteen professional seasons, he scored 30,026 points.

Erving was born in 1950 in Hempstead, N.Y., and learned to play the game on urban playgrounds. By high school he was six feet three inches tall, and his basketball skills earned him a scholarship to the University of Massachusetts. After his junior year, he left college to join the Virginia Squires in the American Basketball Association, where he was an immediate success, averaging 27.3 points per game in his rookie season.

The 1940s brought recognition as a composer, and some of the best known Ellington works: "Chelsea Bridge," "Take the 'A' Train," and "Black, Brown and Beige." The Ellington orchestra appeared in Carnegie Hall and in popular Big Band clubs throughout the United States.

Although the heyday of the big bands was over by the 1950s, Ellington, now with a reputation as a serious composer, continued to compose new works. A triumphant appearance in 1956 at the Newport Jazz Festival was followed by a Time cover story. As in previous years, the orchestra continued to travel in North America and in Europe.

The "King of Swing" earned Grammy Awards, 16 honorary doctorate degrees, and the NAACP's Springarn Medal for achievement by black Americans. Ellington continued to write and perform until his death from lung cancer in 1974.

When the ABA merged with the NBA in 1976, Erving began playing with the Philadelphia 76ers. During eleven seasons with the 76ers, he averaged twenty-two points per game, and was chosen for the All-Star team each year. Erving won the NBA Most Valuable Player award in 1981, and two years later helped lead Philadelphia to the NBA championship. After he retired from the game in 1987, he went back to college to complete his degree, and now devotes time to encouraging African-American youth groups to attend college. Erving was inducted into the Basketball Hall of Fame in Massachussetts in 1993.

MEDGAR EVERS

A symbol of the efforts for African-Americans to gain full equality in the United States, civil rights leader Edgar Wiley Evers was born in 1925 in Decatur, Mississippi. He grew up during a time of intense segregation in the Deep South, when education was not easily available to blacks. In 1946, Evers and his brother Charles tried to vote in their hometown, causing his entire family to be threatened with violence.

After graduating from Alcorn A & M College in 1952, he joined the NAACP. From 1954 to 1963, Evers served as field secretary for the association, traveling throughout Mississippi encouraging African-Americans to register to vote. He also organized African-American boycotts against white-owned firms that practiced racial discrimination, and led demonstrations to integrate public facilities.

Evers became Mississippi's best known champion of civil rights, and as such was a target for white supremacists. On the morning of June 13, 1963, he was shot in the back as he walked up the driveway to his house. Byron De La Beckwith was arrested for Evers's murder and tried twice in 1964. Both times an all-white jury deadlocked, and the charges were dropped. At the urging of Evers's widow, De La Beckwith was brought to trial again in 1994. This time a jury of eight blacks and four whites convicted him.

Julius Erving was a four-time NBA All-Star.

F

JAMES FARMER

Civil rights leader James Leonard Farmer founded the Congress of Racial Equality (CORE) in 1942. The stated purpose of the organization is, "to create a society in which 'race or creed' will be neither an asset or a handicap."

Born in 1920 in Marshall, Texas, Farmer was the son of a Methodist minister. Growing up in the South, he attended mostly segregated schools and earned a degree in chemistry from Wiley College in 1938. From there, Farmer went to Howard University, where he earned a divinity degree in 1941. Upon graduating, he accepted a post as race relations secretary for the Fellowship of Reconciliation, and the following year he and a group at the University of Chicago organized CORE.

As the national director of CORE, Farmer advocated a policy of change through non-violent direct action, such as the 1963 March on Washington for Jobs and Freedom, of which CORE was a sponsor. CORE has organized sit-ins to end segregation in restaurants and on public transportation facilities, has sponsored voter registration drives, and has exerted political pressure on lawmakers by means of large public demonstrations. Farmer resigned as director of CORE in 1966. He wrote several books, and in 1998, President Clinton awarded Farmer the Medal of Freedom for his contributions. Farmer died in 1999.

ELLA FITZGERALD

The "First Lady of Song," jazz singer Ella Fitzgerald, was born in 1918 in Newport News, Virginia. When her father died, shortly after World War I, the family moved to Yonkers, New York. During her teens, Ella entered (and won) many talent contests. Bandleader Chick Webb discovered Fitzgerald in a talent contest at Harlem's Apollo Theater, in 1934. Because she was only 17, Webb and his wife adopted her, becoming her legal guardians. She recorded her first song, "Love and Kisses" with Webb in 1935. The record has disappeared without a trace. In 1936, Fitzgerald began

"scat" singing, which became her signature. The following year she began writing her own songs. Duke Ellington, Nat King Cole and Billie Holiday all recorded songs using Fitzgerald's lyrics. In 1943 she became the youngest person ever admitted to the American Society of Composers.

In 1944 and 1945, Fitzgerald and the Ink Spots had two successive million-selling hits, "Into Each Life Some Rain Must Fall," and Duke Ellington's "I'm Beginning to See the Light." Fitzgerald is the recipient of 12 Grammy Awards, the American Music Award, the National Medal of the Arts, and has been named 'number one female singer' as well as 'best female jazz vocalist' by the International Jazz Critics Poll. Among her greatest recordings are the famous *Gershwin Songbook*, a five record set released in 1958, and the album *The Best Is Yet to Come*, for which she won her 12th Grammy award. Thought to be immortal by her fans, the world was shocked and saddened by Fitzgerald's death in 1996 after a long battle with diabetes.

The "First Lady of Song," Ella Fitzgerald, in 1940.

GEORGE FOREMAN

George Foreman is the oldest boxer ever to hold the heavyweight boxing championship title, which he snagged for the second time in his career in an amazing comeback bout just two months shy of his 46th birthday.

Foreman was born in Marshall, Texas in 1944, and grew up poor in a large family. After dropping out of high school, he entered the Job Corps, where he took up boxing. Foreman won the national amateur heavyweight championship in 1968, and went on to win the heavyweight gold medal at the Olympic Games later the same year. In 1973, he defeated Joe Frazier for the heavyweight championship title, but lost the title a year later to Muhammed Ali.

Foreman retired from boxing in 1977 and returned to Houston, Texas to become an evangelical minister. Ten years later he returned to the ring. In 1991 he challenged heavyweight champion Evander Holyfield for the title, but lost in a 12-round decision. Persisting in his comeback, he won back the title from Moorer in 1994.

Foreman became an instant celebrity, was courted by advertisers and has endorsed everything from hot dogs to mufflers. He also starred in a short-lived television sitcom, *George*. In 1990, Foreman was inducted into the U.S. Olympic Hall of Fame. His autobiography, *By George*, was published in 1995.

ARETHA FRANKLIN

Aretha Franklin at the VH1 Divas Live concert in New York in 1998.

Aretha Franklin was crowned the "Queen of Soul" in 1967 when five of her singles for Atlanta Records sold over a million copies each.

Aretha Louise Franklin was born in 1942 in Memphis, Tennessee. She spent most of her childhood in Detroit, where she and her four siblings were raised by their father, who was a well-known evangelist preacher and singer. At the age of 14, she made her first solo recording as a gospel singer for Chess Records. A year later she became pregnant, and dropped out of high school to have the baby. When she turned 18, Franklin decided to move to New York in hopes of becoming a successful blues singer.

In 1960, Columbia records signed Franklin to a five-year contract. She became well known among jazz audiences and black consumers in the early 1960s, but really wanted to branch out. When she signed with Atlantic in 1965, Aretha had changed her style to appeal to fans of both popular music and rhythm and blues. Between 1967 and 1969, Franklin won four Grammy awards. She produced at least one million-selling song each year between 1967 and 1973. During the 1970s, she earned six more Grammys.

Franklin was the first woman inducted into the Rock and Roll Hall of Fame, and in 1994 she was awarded the Grammy for Lifetime Achievement. In thirty years she made thirty five albums and had seventeen number one R & B singles, including her best known, "Respect," along with "Chain of Fools," "Ain't Nothing Like the Real Thing," "Don't Play That Song For Me," and "Master of Eyes."

JOE FRAZIER

Championship boxer Joe Frazier's three heavyweight title bouts with Muhammed Ali rank among the greatest matches in boxing history.

Joseph Frazier was born in Beaufort, South Carolina in 1944. He began his boxing career in the early 1960's in Philadelphia. Frazier won the gold medal in the heavyweight

Joe Frazier, March 1989.

class (now called super heavyweight) at the 1964 Olympic Games in Tokyo, recording three knockouts in four bouts. He turned professional in 1965. Frazier gained the WBA heavyweight championship title by defeating Jimmy Ellis in 1970, who had become WBA heavyweight champ when Muhammed Ali had been stripped of the title in 1967 for refusing to participate in the U.S. Army draft.

By 1971, when Ali was cleared to fight again, Frazier met him in a championship bout in New York City. The fight was one of the most publicized events in the history if the sport. After a hard 15-round battle, Frazier retained his title in a unanimous decision. In 1975, Frazier lost the WBA heavyweight title to George Foreman. He retired in 1976 with a career record of 32 wins (27 by knockout), 4 losses and one draw. In 1989, Frazier was inducted into the U.S. Olympic Hall of Fame, and the following year was inducted into the International Boxing Hall of Fame. His autobiography, *Smokin' Joe*, was published in 1996.

WALT FRAZIER

Basketball player Walt Frazier was born in 1945 in Atlanta, Georgia. After attending Southern Illinois University, he joined the New York Knickerbockers in 1967. During his ten-year career with the Knicks, Frazier was the all-time leader in assists with 4,791, and his outstanding ball handling skills led him to be primarily responsible for both the team's offense and defense. He was named to the National Basketball Association's All-Defensive Squad for eight consecutive years, and twice he was voted best defensive player in the NBA. In 1974 and 75, Frazier was named MVP of both All-Star games. Frazier retired from basketball in 1980, and was inducted into the Basketball Hall of Fame in 1987.

MORGAN FREEMAN

Actor Morgan Freeman was born in 1937 in Greenwood, Mississippi. He was first introduced to acting at the age of eight, when he performed in his school play. After four years in the Air Force, Freeman took acting classes at Los Angeles City College. He performed in small roles locally, until he moved to New York in the 1960s. Freeman's first important role came in 1967 when he starred in the off-Broadway production, *Nigger Lovers*. His performance led to his Broadway debut later that year in an all-black version of *Hello Dolly!*, starring Pearl Bailey.

During the 1970s, Freeman was a regular on the Public Television children's program "The Electric Company." More theater roles followed in the 1980s, earning Freeman a Tony award and two Obie awards for his various Broadway performances. In 1987, Freeman was cast in the Broadway play *Driving Miss Daisy*. He won an Obie award for his portrayal of Hoke, the chauffeur of a wealthy white woman in the American South. When he reenacted his role for the movie version of the play in 1989, he won an Academy Award for Best Actor. The same year, he appeared in the highly successful movie *Glory*, for which he also earned an Oscar nomination. In 1995, Freeman was again nominated for an Academy Award for his role in *The Shawshank Redemption*.

Walt Frazier was inducted into the Basketball Hall of Fame in 1987.

ZINA GARRISON

At the peak of her career, tennis player Zina Garrison was one of the top professional athletes in the world. She was the first black woman to play on Wimbledon's center court since Althea Gibson, in 1958.

Garrison was born in 1963 in Houston, Texas. She was the youngest of seven children raised by her widowed mother. Zina began playing tennis at local public courts as a child, and by the age of sixteen was playing in national tournaments. In 1981, at the age of seventeen, she was the first black player to win the junior singles championship at Wimbledon. She also won the junior singles title at the U.S. Open, and as a result was named top female amateur athlete in tennis by the U.S. Olympic Committee. Garrison won more U. S. Tennis Association junior singles titles than any other African-American player. She turned professional and was ranked 16th in the world at the end of 1982.

By 1987, Garrison was ranked number nine in the world. At the 1988 Olympic Games in Seoul, South Korea, she took home a bronze medal in singles, and a gold in doubles with her partner, Pam Shriver. In 1989, Garrison defeated Chris Evert at the U.S. Open during the last tournament of Evert's career. Garrison maintained her top ten ranking among women tennis players in the world from 1983–1991.

MARCUS GARVEY

Marcus Garvey was responsible for organizing one of the largest mass movements of black Americans ever, the Black Nationalists. Over a million people participated in his "Back to Africa" emigration effort to form a national homeland with self-government.

Garvey was born in Jamaica in 1887, the youngest of eleven children. In 1912, he studied in London, where he first met and became interested in Africans. Returning to Jamaica in 1914, he founded the Universal Negro Improvement Association (UNIA). The organization worked for black emigration to Africa, and helped promote racial pride, education, and black business activity. Garvey settled in New York in 1916, and started the black weekly, *Negro World*, which soon had 500,000 readers in the United States. By 1920, UNIA had become a major organization. At its first convention in New York City later that year, Garvey outlined his plans to build an African nation-state before a crowd of more than 250,000. He claimed the UNIA had a membership of more than 2 million at its peak.

In the years following the convention, the UNIA began to decline in popularity, and Garvey suffered a series of financial disasters. He was jailed in 1925 on charges of mail fraud, and was deported to Jamaica when his sentence was commuted two years later. He moved to England in 1935, where he died in 1940 at the age of 53.

MARVIN GAYE

Recording artist Marvin Gaye was born in Washington, D.C. in 1939. He was the son of a minister and began singing in church as a child. By the 1950s he was singing as a member of the doo-wop group the Moonglows, and in 1960 was discovered by Berry Gordy, Jr., the head of Motown Records. In 1962, Gaye recorded the first of what would be more than 20 hit records for Motown. His pairing with some of Motown's top female singers such as Mary Wells, Kim Weston, and later Diana Ross, skyrocketed his career. His partnership with Tammi Terrell produced hits like "Ain't No Mountain High Enough" and "Ain't Nothing Like the Real Thing."

In 1971, Gaye had begun to write, arrange and produce his own work, and this was the time he began putting out songs that dealt with major issues of the day such as "What's Going On," and "Mercy Mercy Me." Later hits included "Lets Get It On" (1973) and "Sexual Healing," which won a Grammy Award in 1982.

Gaye was shot to death by his father during a violent quarrel in his home in Los Angeles in 1984. His father was sentenced to five years in prison for voluntary manslaughter.

ALTHEA GIBSON

Althea Gibson was not only the first black woman ever to reach the top ranks of professional tennis, she was the first person to break the color barrier in professional tennis. Her 1950 integration of tennis occurred at the same time that Jackie Robinson was allowed to play in major league baseball.

Althea Gibson was born in 1927 in South Carolina, but she was raised in Harlem, where she learned to play paddle tennis. In 1942, she began to receive coaching at the Interracial Cosmopolitan Tennis Club, and a year later won the New York State Negro Girls Singles Title. She went on to win the National Negro Girls Singles championship, and in 1948 moved to the Women's division. Gibson played tennis and basketball during her college years at Texas A & M, and in 1950 became the first black to play at Forest Hills. The following year she became the first black to play at Wimbledon.

In 1957, Gibson won the Wimbledon singles title, and teamed with Darlene Hard to win the doubles championship as well. She won the U.S. Open Women's Singles title in 1957 and 1958. Both years, Gibson was named the Associated Press Woman Athlete of the Year. In 1958 she published her autobiography, *I Always Wanted to Be Somebody*.

Dizzy Gillespie in December, 1955.

DIZZY GILLESPIE

As one of the originators of the most revolutionary movement in jazz during the 1940s, Dizzy Gilespie became an icon of the phenomenon known as "Bop," a fast-paced, free-ranging style that changed the face of jazz forever. John Birks ("Dizzy") Gillespie was born in South Carolina in 1917. He received his early musical training in South Carolina, and moved to Philadelphia in 1935 to receive more professional experience. After touring Europe in 1939, he returned to New York to play with Cab Calloway. It was during this time that Gillespie began to develop his career as a composer and arranger.

In the 1940s, Gillespie and Charlie Parker, together with other jazz musicians, established a new approach to jazz known as "bop," a modern style developed in New York's Minton's Playhouse, using unusual chords and irregular rhythms. With his technically inventive playing, rapid with sustained high notes, Gillespie set the standard for other bebop trumpeters. Although he usually led small bands, his was the first bebop big band, in the 1940s. Gillespie toured Europe, the Middle East and Latin America with big bands and quintets, subsidized by the United States State Department. In 1979, Gillespie published *To Be or Not to Bop: Memoirs*. He died in 1993 in Englewood, New Jersey.

NIKKI GIOVANNI

Poet Nikki Giovanni first won acclaim in the 1960s during the rise of the black literary renaissance. Called the "Princess of Black Poetry", the revolutionary themes in her work captured the spirit of the times.

Nikki Giovanni was born Yolande Cornelia Giovanni, Jr. in 1943 in Tennessee. While attending Fisk University from 1960 to 1964, she became a civil rights activist and helped organize the campus chapter of the Student Nonviolent Coordinating Committee (SNCC). After graduating, Giovanni became involved with the Black Power movement.

WHOOPIE GOLDBERG

One of America's most popular entertainers, Whoopie Goldberg overcame poverty, drug addiction and welfare to achieve super-stardom in film, television and theater.

Goldberg was born Caryn Johnson in New York on November 13th, 1955. She was raised by her mother in a housing project on the Lower West Side on Manhattan. Goldberg's talent was already apparent by the age of eight, when she joined the Helena Rubenstein Children's Theater at the Hudson Guild. At the age of 17, she dropped out of High School for the Performing Arts, dispirited by her poor academic performance, but unaware that she suffered from dyslexia.

Goldberg soon became involved in the youth culture of the 1960s, and developed a drug problem. After checking into a treatment center, she became romantically involved with her drug counselor. They were married, and Goldberg gave birth to a daughter, Alexandrea, at the age of 18. Only a year later, they divorced, and Goldberg moved back in with her mother.

In 1974, Goldberg moved to the West Coast to pursue her childhood ambition to act. While performing with the San Diego Repertory Company, she worked at odd jobs, including styling hair at a mortuary and laying bricks. When Goldberg joined the "Black Street Hawkeyes" dramatic troupe from Berkeley, California in 1980, she began to develop a following. Director Mike Nichols spotted her performance with the troupe in New York, and signed her to do a one-woman show on Broadway. When *Whoopie Direct From Broadway* opened in 1984, it was a smash hit at the box office, and the recorded version won a Grammy Award for Best Comedy Album. The same year, Stephen Spielberg cast her in the acclaimed film, *The Color Purple*, for which she won a Golden Globe Award and an Academy Award nomination.

After appearing in a number of films in the late 1980's, Goldberg's performance as Oda Mae Brown in the film *Ghost* earned her an Academy Award in 1991. In the years following, she appeared in several films, including *Sister Act*, and its sequel, *Sister Act II*, *Boys on the Side*, and *How Stella Got Her Groove Back*.

Goldberg has made many television appearances, including becoming the first woman in the history of the ceremonies to host the Academy Awards in 1994. She has received the People's Choice Award for Favorite Comedy Movie Actress several times.

After concentrating on her movie career for ten years, Goldberg returned to the stage in a broadway revival of *A Funny Thing Happened on the Way to the Forum*, playing a role originally written for and acted by a white male. She hosted the Academy Awards ceremonies again in 1996 and 1999.

Goldberg has always used her stardom to promote humanitarian causes, dedicating herself to women's rights, AIDS research and drug abuse prevention. Her most notable public service effort, *Comic Relief*, has raised millions of dollars to aid homeless people in the United States.

Whoopie Goldberg in 1992.

A reflection of her strong activism can be found in the three books of poetry she published between 1968 and 1970: *Black Feeling, Black Talk* (1968), *Black Judgement* (1968) and *Re: Creation* (1970). Her early work was enormously popular, and she became—according to critic Mozella G. Mitchell—"one of the three leading figures of the new black poetry between 1968 and 1971," along with Sonia Sanchez and Don L. Lee.

After the birth of her son in 1969, Giovanni began to focus on family-oriented themes and positive images for black children. In 1970, she established her own publishing company, Niktom (named for herself and her son Thomas), for the purpose of creating literature directed specifically to a black audience, celebrating the positive features of black life. She has published more than ten volumes of poetry, including some for children. In addition to teaching college, Giovanni continues to write, lecture, appear on television, and to give poetry readings nationwide and abroad. She has received numerous honorary degrees and was named "Woman of the Year" by three major magazines in the early 1970s—*Ebony*, *Mademoiselle* and *The Ladies' Home Journal*—and won a National Book Award for her poetry collection, *Gemini*. Giovanni and has been elected to the Ohio Women's Hall of Fame, where she lives.

BERRY GORDY, Jr.

As the founder of Motown Records, Berry Gordy, Jr. played a major role in bringing African-American music styles to the forefront of American popular culture.

Gordy was born in Detroit, Michigan in 1929. As a teenager he was mainly interested in music and boxing, dropping out of high school his junior year to become a featherweight. His boxing career was cut short when he was drafted into the U.S. Army in 1951. After being discharged two years later, Gordy opened a record store in Detroit. In 1959, he borrowed $800 from his parents and started his own record company. Working with talented songwriters and producers, Gordy created the "Motown sound," a combination of rhythm and blues, with ele-

ments derived from gospel music, driven by an engaging beat.

By 1974, Motown had become the most successful black-owned company in the United States, with annual sales of more than $50 million. Gordy's roster of performers included the Marvelettes, the Supremes, the Four Tops, Smokey Robinson and the Miracles, Martha Reeves, Mary Wells, Al Green, the Temptations, Stevie Wonder, the Jackson Five, and others. In 1988, Motown was sold to the Music Corporation of America for $61 million. Gordy has created a Motown museum, housed in the original Motown offices on Grand Boulevard in Detroit. He was inducted into the Rock and Roll Hall of Fame in Cleveland in 1988.

EARL GRAVES, Sr.

In the early 1970s, publishing pioneer Earl Graves, Sr. emerged as a leading authority on black entrepreneurship with his popular magazine *Black Enterprise*, which focused primarily on effective solutions to problems facing the black business community. The magazine has become widely accepted as an authority on the progress of minority owned and operated businesses and minorities in business, while advocating social responsibility to its black, middle class readership.

Graves was born in Brooklyn, New York in 1935. He graduated from Morgan State College, a historically black college in Baltimore, in 1958. In 1965, Graves joined the staff of Senator Robert F. Kennedy as an administrative assistant. After Senator Kennedy's assassination, Graves left public service and organized Earl Graves Associates, a consulting firm on urban affairs and black economic development. When *Black Enterprise* was published in 1970, it was the first business magazine directed to the black middle class, providing insight into financial planning and investment, as well as guidance and assistance to African-American business owners in managing their ventures. The magazine enjoys a wide readership outside the black community as well.

CLARA HALE

Mother Clara Hale at Hale House, 1985.

As problems associated with drug abuse hit New York City's Harlem neighborhood in the 1960s, "Mother" Hale was called upon to help. Hale was already well known in the community for her work as a foster-parent and child-care giver. In 1969, Hale's daughter Lorraine sent to her a cocaine-addicted black mother who was wandering the streets with her baby. This was the beginning of Hale House, the first—and only known program in the U.S.—devoted to infants born addicted to illegal drugs. She soon had more than twenty babies of heroin-addicted women in her apartment.

Clara McBride Hale was born in 1904, in Philadelphia, Pennsylvania, and was orphaned at sixteen. After graduation from high school, she married Thomas Hale and moved to Brooklyn, New York. She was left to raise their three children alone after she became a widow in 1932. In order to earn money, she began taking care of other people's children, and by 1940 she had become an official foster parent and daycare giver for working mothers.

Using funds from private and public sources, Mother Hale, also known as the "Mother Teresa of New York," put together a small staff, and in the mid 1970s, Hale House in Harlem became an officially licensed childcare facility for babies born addicted to drugs. As the AIDS epidemic exploded ten years later, Hale House shifted its focus to care for AIDS-infected babies and children.

In 1985, President Ronald Reagan praised Mother Hale as an American hero in his State of the Union Address. In 1987, she was awarded two of the Salvation Army's highest honors, the Booth Community Service Award and the Leonard H. Carter Humanitarian Award.

Although Hale died of a stroke in 1992, her legacy continues under the leadership of her daughter. Each year a benefit dinner is held in New York City to celebrate Hale's achievements, where worthy individuals receive Mother Hale Awards for Caring. The proceeds from the event help to sustain Hale House.

ALEX HALEY

Alex Haley was best known for his pioneering work, *Roots: The Saga of an American Family*. The 1976 book, which traces the story of his family from its roots in Africa through slave times until emancipation, was a huge international bestseller. Almost 2 million people watched the TV version of *Roots*, an eight-part series, in 1977.

Born Alex Palmer Haley in Ithaca, New York in 1921, he was the son of a professor and a teacher. After serving in the U.S. Coast Guard for 20 years, Haley left to become a free-lance writer in 1959. He wrote numerous articles during his freelance career, and in 1965, partnered with Malcolm X to write the *Autobiography of Malcolm X*.

Both the Pulitzer Prize Committee and the National Book Award Committee gave *Roots* special citations in 1977. Vernon Jordan, then director of the Nation Urban League, called the television *Roots* "the single most spectacular educational experience in race relations in America." In the same year, Haley was awarded the NAACP's Spingarn Medal for outstanding achievement by a black American. He died in 1992 in Seattle.

Queen: The Story of an American Family was published after his death. The novel was a saga of the Haley family, from the emigration of Haley's Irish great, great grandfather to America's South, his great grandfather's love of a slave, and the birth of his grandmother, Queen. Haley tells the story of Queen, a free woman after the Civil War. In a world where she looks white but is regarded as a black, Queen searches for her identity and for a better life in a still unequal society.

LIONEL HAMPTON

Born in Kentucky in 1913, Lionel Hampton played the snare drum as a child, beginning his musical life in marching bands. As a young musician playing in a band with Louis Armstrong, he began experimenting with the vibraphone, an amplified xylophone not associated with jazz at the time. Hampton made his first vibraphone recording with Armstrong in 1930.

After being hired by Benny Goodman in 1936, Hampton became one of the mainstays of the Goodman organization, playing in small combos as well as the main band. He formed his own band in 1941. Due to changes in the musical climate over time, Hampton dropped his band and formed a sextet in the 1960s. The group was well received and played in major clubs throughout the U.S. and Europe. Hampton is best known for making the vibraphone an effective instrument of jazz and giving it a secure place among the other percussion instruments in a jazz ensemble. His recording of "Flying Home," done in 1942, remains a classic of the big band jazz era.

W.C. HANDY

William Christopher Handy is considered by many to be the "Father of the Blues" due to his pioneering role in making the folk blues of African-Americans accessible to the general public.

Handy was born in Alabama in 1873 to former slaves. His parents provided him with organ lessons but forbade him to play secular music, encouraging him to play only sacred. While in high school, he defied his parents and joined a local band to play coronet. At the age of 18, Handy became an itinerant musician, touring with his own bands playing rag time and minstrel music.

In 1914, along with fellow musician Harry Pace, Handy created a music publishing company, Pace and Handy Music Company, Publishers, and began issuing his own compositions. His songs introduced "folk blues," a type of blues distinct from the more familiar spiritual and work songs of Southern blacks at the time. The publishing company moved to New York where it led the field in introducing the music of African-American songwriters to the public. Handy published *Negro Authors and Composers of the United States* (1935), and *Unsung Americans Sung* (1944), along with other books of music as well as his own autobiography, *Father of the Blues*, in 1941. Handy died in 1958 in New York.

LORRAINE HANSBERRY

Lorraine Vivian Hansberry's award-winning play, *Raisin in the Sun*, was the first play written by an African-American woman to be produced on Broadway, opening in 1958.

Hansberry was born in Chicago in 1930, the daughter of a prominent businessman who had founded one of Chicago's first black banks. Her childhood was the inspiration for *Raisin*, a story based upon the time her father tried to move the family to an all-white neighborhood and was blocked by Illinois state law.

After attending University of Wisconsin for two years, Hansberry moved to New York and began writing short stories, poems and plays. She devoted a full year to writing *Raisin*, which met with instant success and was subsequently made into a movie. In 1964, Hansberry had a second play on Broadway, *The Sign in Sidney Brustein's Window*, which was still running when she died of cancer in 1965, at the age of 34. After her death, her husband, Robert Nemiroff, compiled and edited her autobiographical work and published *To Be Young, Gifted, and Black*, which was also made into a play.

DOROTHY HEIGHT

Dorothy Irene Height is best known for her leadership roles with the Young Women's Christian Association (YWCA) and the National Council of Negro Women (NCNW). For nearly half a century she has been a crusader for equality and human rights for all people.

Height was born in 1912 in Richmond, Virginia. She earned bachelor's and master's degrees from New York University, and also studied at the New York School of Social Work. Her civil rights activities began during the depression when she joined the Harlem branch of the YWCA, the beginning of a two-decade association with the organization. In 1957 Height became the president of the NCNW, serving into the 1990s. Working closely with Dr. Martin Luther King, among other black leaders, she participated in virtually all the major civil and human rights events of the 1960s. In addition to receiving over twenty honorary degrees, she has served as a consultant on African affairs to the United States secretary of state. In 1978, Height became the first woman to receive the Distinguished Service Award from the National Newspaper Publishers Association. President Reagan presented Height with the Citizen's Medal award for distinguished service in 1989.

FLETCHER HENDERSON

Musical arranger and bandleader Fletcher Henderson is generally thought to be the first jazz musician to use written arrangements. His orchestral arrangements, particularly the ones he wrote for Benny Goodman's band in the 1930s, became the foundation and architecture of "swing."

Fletcher Hamilton Henderson was born in Georgia in 1897, and moved to New York in 1920 to study chemistry. To earn extra money, he took a job at the first black-owned and operated record company, Black Swan, as house pianist and musical director. He gradually moved away from chemistry, after a band he played with began playing at the Roseland Ballroom in Broadway in the mid-1920s.

Henderson's own band helped to launch some of the greatest stars of the day, including Louis Armstrong, Coleman Hawkins and Benny Carter. In 1933, Henderson began writing full-time for his band. It was his notable talent for arranging music that led him to become the major innovator of swing. Henderson continued to write music and lead bands, although his greatest success was with his band in the 1920s. He died in 1952 in New York.

JIMI HENDRIX

Widely revered as one of the most influential rock guitarists of the 1960s, Jimi Hendrix redefined the sound of the electric guitar and changed the course of music from jazz fusion to heavy metal.

Born Johnny Allen Hendrix in Seattle in 1942, he was renamed James Marshall by his father four years later. As a teenager in the late 1950s, Henrix began playing in local bands in Seattle. After a twenty-six month stint in the Air Force, he arrived on the Nashville rhythm and blues scene, performing under the name Jimi James as back up for acts such as Little Richard, Ike and Tina Turner, and the Isley Brothers. In 1964, Hendrix moved to New York where he formed the group "Jimi James and the Blue Flames." After being discovered by producer and manager Chris Chandler, the former bassist with the Animals, he left for England where he formed the Jimi Hendrix Experience in 1966. A year later the group released the groundbreaking album *Are You Experienced*.

When he was invited to perform at the Monterey Pop Festival in 1967, Hendrix's dazzling, exhuberant peformance, which climaxed with him setting his guitar on fire, made him an instant success in the U.S. After two successful tours in 1968, the Experience released two consecutive hit albums: *Axis: Bold as Love* and *Electric Ladyland*. After the group broke up in 1969, Hendrix began performing with new musicians and made a memorable appearance at the Woodstock Festival, where he performed his unique version of the "Star Spangled Banner." He then formed a new group, Band of Gypsies, and recorded two more albums, *Band of Gypsies* and *Cry of Love*. By this point, Hendrix's musical innovations were influencing the world of rock music.

In 1970 Hendrix moved back to England, where the pressures of his grueling tour and recording schedule were beginning to take their toll. His last major performance took place at the Isle of Wight Festival in August of 1970. On September 18th, Hendrix was found dead in his hotel room, as a result of a mixture of barbiturates and alcohol. His death is believed to have been accidental. Hendrix was inducted into the Rock and Roll Hall of Fame in 1992.

Jimi Hendrix performing at the Isle of Wight Festival in 1970.

GREGORY HINES

Tony Award-winning dancer Gregory Hines has been a dedicated advocate for recognition of black dance throughout his career on stage, in film and in television.

Hines was born in 1946 in New York and began dancing professionally at the age of five with his brother, Maurice, as the Hines Kids. As teenagers the duo performed as the Hines brothers until their father joined their act and they became known as Hines, Hines and Dad.

In 1978, Hines landed his first part as a tap dancer in a Broadway show, beginning a long dance career on Broadway that has earned him several Tony Award nominations. Hines made the transition into

Gregory Hines at the Distinguished Artists Awards Ceremony in 1997.

film, starting with dance roles and working his way toward being a dramatic actor. His films included *The Cotton Club* (1984), *White Nights* (1985), *Running Scared* (1985), *Off Limits* (1988), *Tap* (1989), *White Man's Burden* (1994) and *Dead Air* (1995). In addition, he has made numerous public appearances to celebrate tap dancing, including the television documentary, *Tappin': The Making of Tap*, in 1989. Hines also appeared in the television special, "Motown Returns to the Apollo," for which he won an Emmy nomination. He has received the Dance Educators Award, the Theater World Award, and in 1992 received a Tony award for best actor in a musical for his role as Jelly Roll Morton in *Jelly's Last Jam*.

GEOFFREY HOLDER

Geoffrey Holder was born in Trinidad in 1930. After forming his own dance company in 1950 and touring the Caribbean, he made his Broadway debut in 1954. He was a solo dancer with the Metropolitan Opera Company from 1956 to 1957, then made his dramatic debut in the play *Waiting for Godot*. For Dance Theatre of Harlem, he wrote the music, choreographed, and designed the costumes for three ballets and created the costumes and sets for *Firebird*.

Between the years 1956 and 1960, his dancing continued as he performed with his own troupe, the Geoffrey Holder Dance Company, in New York City. In 1968, his masterpiece, *The Prodigal Prince*, for which he wrote the music, did the choreography, and designed the costumes, was performed by the Alvin Ailey American Dance Theatre at City Center in New York.

During the 1960s and 1970s, Holder took multiple roles as director, choreographer and costume designer for several stage productions, including *The Wiz*, for which he won two Tony Awards in 1975. His film credits include *Dr. Doolittle* (1967), *Live and Let Die* (1973) and *Annie* (1982). In 1957 Holder received a Guggenheim Fellowship in painting, and has displayed his work in galleries from San Juan, Puerto Rico to Washington, D.C. He has also written and illustrated two books: *Black Gods, Green Islands*, and *Caribbean Cookbook*. Holder became familiar to television audiences through his appearances in Seven-Up commercials in the 1970s.

Geoffrey Holder in 1954.

BILLIE HOLIDAY

Billie Holiday, known to her fans as "Lady Day," was born in Baltimore, Maryland in 1915. Holiday survived a childhood of destitution, abuse and separation from her mother. She moved to New York and began her career as a singer in 1931, while still a young girl. In 1933, she cut her first record with Benny Goodman, and continued to establish her reputation throughout the 1930s with a series of records made with Teddy Wilson. She also sang with the bands of Count Basie and Artie Shaw. Some of her best known songs include "Strange Fruit" and "God Bless the Child," which depict the harsh reality of Southern lynchings and personal alienation.

Holiday had a troubled life, including a period of addiction to drugs and alcohol. In her 1956 autobiography, *Lady Sings the Blues*, Holiday writes, "All dope can do is kill you

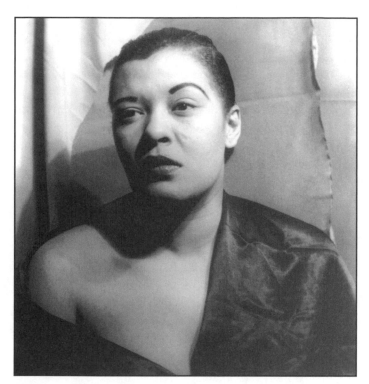

Billie Holiday in 1949.

—and kill you the long, slow, hard way." Her last performance was captured on film and broadcast on television, in *The Sound of Jazz*, in 1957. Billie Holiday remains a powerful force in music today, decades after her untimely death in 1959 at the age of 44.

LENA HORNE

The glamorous Lena Horne was the first African-American of either sex to be given a long-term contract at a major Hollywood studio, Metro-Goldwyn-Mayer.

Horne was born in Brooklyn, New York in 1917. In 1933 she joined the chorus line at the famous Cotton Club in Harlem, then joined Charlie Barnett's band as a singer in 1939. She made her first records with Barnett, and also worked at New York's Café Society Downtown. The majority of Horne's notable Hollywood films took place in the 1940s, including *Panama Hattie* (1942), *Cabbie in the Sky* (1943), *Stormy Weather* (1943), and *Meet Me in Las Vegas* (1956). She went on to make frequent television appearances, sing in clubs and make concert appearances; her best known songs were "Stormy Weather," "The Lady is a Tramp," and "Mad About the Boy."

In 1981, she opened a one-woman show called *Lena Horne: The Lady And Her Music*, which earned her a special Tony Award. In December of the same year she received

New York City's highest cultural award, the Handel Medallion. She has headlined at all of the major nightclubs in the U.S. and continues to entertain on stage and in television. In 1997, PBS broadcast the documentary, *Lena Horne: In Her Own Voice*.

Lena Horne in 1987.

WHITNEY HOUSTON

Popular singer, model and actress, Whitney Houston dominated the pop charts during the 1980s and into the 90s. Houston began her singing career at the age of 11, as a member of the New Hope Baptist Choir in East Orange, New Jersey. As a teenager she became a fashion model, appearing on magazine covers from *Glamour* to *Cosmopolitan*. During this time she continued seeking a career in music, singing backup with her mother, Cissy Houston, for the Neville Brothers, Lou Rawls and Chaka Kahn (Cissy Houston also sang back-up for Aretha Franklin, Dionne Warwick, Bette Midler, and Herbie Mann.)

In 1985 she released her first album, *Whitney Houston*, which sold more than sixteen million copies. It includes her hits, "Greatest Love of All," and "Saving All My Love for You," which won Houston a Grammy award for best female pop vocalist.

Her second album, *Whitney*, released in 1987, won four American Music awards. Four singles from the album reached number one on the Billboard chart. In 1992, Houston made her acting debut in the film, *The Bodyguard*. The first single from the soundtrack, "I Will Always Love You," spent 14 straight weeks at the top of the pop chart. According to *Billboard* magazine, Houston has set a record for the most times spent at the top of the charts. *The Bodyguard* soundtrack won Houston seven American Music Awards; four Grammy awards, including record of the year, album of the year, and best female pop performance; two Soul Train Music awards; four NAACP Image awards; and the National Association of Black Owned Broadcasters' lifetime achievement award.

LANGSTON HUGHES

Langston Hughes in 1936.

Langston Hughes, one of the earliest writers of the Harlem Renaissance, was a prolific writer of poetry, songs, novels, plays, histories, biographies and essays. Born in 1902 in Joplin, Missouri, in grammar school he was the class poet, and in high school he published stories and poetry in his school's monthly magazine.

Hughes's poem, "The Negro Speaks of Rivers," was published in 1921 in *The Crisis*, the magazine of the NAACP. As a part of the Harlem Renaissance, the black cultural movement of the 1920s that initiated a new black literature, Hughes was one of a group of writers who used the ordinary experiences of black, working people as the subject of their work.

Hughes's writing was known for its identity with the blues, rhythms of jazz, use of black speech, as well as including social protest, particularly in dealing with race relations. His work helped change the face of both African-American and American literature. Hughes received numerous awards, including one from the Academy of Arts and Letters, as well as the NAACP's Spingarn Award for acheivement by a black American. In 1961, he was elected to the National Institute of Arts and Letters.

Hughes remained an active writer, publishing and touring through the 1950s and 1960s, right up until the time of his death in 1967 in New York City.

ZORA NEALE HURSTON

Zora Neale Hurston's work as a major literary figure of the Harlem Renaissance has inspired many of today's writers, particularly Alice Walker, who helped to "rediscover" Hurston.

Hurston was born in 1891, and was raised in the all-black town of Eatonville, Florida. Her experiences growing up in a racially isolated community served as a theme in much of her later literary work. Her short story, "Drenched in Light," focuses on a young girl much like Hurston herself, with suggestions of an all-black world. When Hurston moved to New York in 1925, she became acquainted with other black writers and artists, like herself, who were publishing new views of black cultural life. She and Langston Hughes, together, saw themselves as rebels with a vision of a black life that was free from racial pressure. The two were at the center of the Harlem Renaissance literary movement of the 1920s.

In 1937, Hurston published *Her Eyes Were Watching God*, the novel thought to be her best work of fiction. In addition to many novels, short stories and plays, Hurston also produced scholarly publications. She was a trained anthropologist who worked and traveled in the Caribbean and Central America. At the time of her death in 1960, Hurston's career had suffered a steep decline, and she was destitute and isolated. Her work remains an important source of black pride and the black female experience, and her studies of black culture continue to be influential.

JESSE JACKSON

As a minister, civil rights activist and political candidate, Jesse Jackson has become the most visible African American leader since Martin Luther King, Jr. He was the first person to inspire people to consider the possibility of a black President of the United States.

Jesse Louis Jackson was born in 1941 in Greenville, South Carolina. It was in college that he first became committed to the civil rights movement, organizing campus sit-ins and directing the southeastern operations of the Congress for Racial Equality. After graduating in 1964 with a degree in sociology, Jackson attended the Chicago Theological Seminary, where he became an ordained Baptist minister. In 1965 he joined Dr. Martin Luther King's Southern Christian Leadership Conference, and served as the program's executive director from 1967 to 1971.

After the assassination of King in 1968, Jackson moved away from the SCLC and began his own program, People United to Save Humanity. PUSH focused on promoting black economic progress and political participation, as well as fighting drugs, teen pregnancy, and violence in the black community.

In the 1980s, Jesse Jackson became a political candidate and made two bids for the Democratic nomination for president. After making a good, albeit unsuccessful, showing in 1984, he tried again in 1988. This time he was a serious contender and with his multiracial organization, the Rainbow Coalition, won nine state primaries and 7 million of 23 million votes cast. Although he once again fell short of the nomination, Jackson had become a major force in the nation's political life, and an important player on the world scene. Jackson continues to write, speak and lead protests for social change. In 1993, he was awarded the Martin Luther King, Jr. Nonviolent Peace Prize.

During the Kosovo crisis in 1999, Jackson received a commendation from the U.S. Senate for winning the release of three American soldiers captured in Yugoslavia.

MAHALIA JACKSON

Known to many as the Queen of Gospel Song, Mahalia Jackson can be credited for bringing gospel music to an unprecedented level of popularity both in the U.S. and abroad.

Born in 1911 in New Orleans, Louisiana, Jackson was raised by parents who forbade her to sing anything but religious music in the home. After moving to Chicago as a teenager, she became the lead singer in the Greater Salem Baptist Church choir.

Jackson began her professional career in 1930 as a member of the gospel quintet, the Johnson Singers. In 1945 she recorded gospel music's first million-selling record, "Move on Up a Little Higher," which made her famous in Europe and America. In 1954 Jackson became the first gospel singer to be featured on a radio program, and she inspired many in the civil rights movement with her song, "We Shall Overcome." In the 1960s, Jackson performed at the White House as well as at London's Albert Hall. Not only did she sing at Martin Luther King's 1963 March on Washington, but also at his funeral ceremony in 1968.

When Jackson died of a heart condition in Chicago in 1972, 45,000 mourners gathered at her funeral to pay their respects.

Jesse Jackson, shown here in August 1991.

MICHAEL JACKSON

Beginning as a child star, through his reign as "King of Pop" in the 1980s, Michael Jackson has gathered the largest following of any African-American singer in the history of popular music.

Michael "Jacko" Jackson in Rotterdam, Holland, in 1988.

Michael Joseph Jackson was born in 1958 in Gary, Indiana, the fifth of nine children. At the age of six, Michael, along with four of his brothers, began performing as the Jackson Five. After signing with Motown Records in 1969, the group became an instant success with young people of all races. During their years at Motown, the Jackson Five recorded 13 consecutive top 20 singles, such as "ABC," "The Love You Save," and "I'll Be There." Michael also had a separate solo contract with Motown, and began to move away from his brothers professionally as he approached adulthood. Together with producer Quincy Jones, Jackson recorded the solo album *Off the Wall* in 1979, which sold more than 10 million copies. Two years later, the pair teamed up again to release the biggest selling album of all time, *Thriller*, which contained 6 top-ten hits and sold 40 million copies worldwide. Jackson's music videos for the singles from *Thriller* made inroads for artists of all colors and set a new standard for music videos.

In 1985, Jackson co-wrote the song "We Are the World," with Lionel Richie, as part of a campaign to aid famine in Africa. His next two albums, *Bad*, released in 1987 and *Dangerous*, released in 1991, sold millions of copies, although they didn't quite reach the success for *Thriller*. In 1994, Jackson married Lisa Marie Presely, daughter of famed pop singer Elvis, although they divorced after 18 months. He and wife Debbie Rowe, whom he married in 1996, have a son, Prince Michael Jackson, Jr. and a daughter named Paris Michael Katherine Jackson.

JUDITH JAMISON

The first African-American woman to direct a major dance company, Judith Jamison was born in 1944 in Philadelphia and began dancing at the age of six. She was discovered by Agnes DeMille at a master class and her professional dance career began when she joined the Alvin Ailey Dance Theater in 1965. As a principal dancer with the

Judith Jamison in "Cry."

company, Jamison performed a wide range of black roles especially choreographed for her by Ailey, including "Cry." In the 1980s she performed in the Broadway musical *Sophisticated Ladies*, with Gregory Hines. Her dance career included guest performances with American Ballet Theater, Harkness Ballet, San Francisco Ballet, and many European dance companies.

After her career as a dancer, Jamison went on to establish her own dance company, the Jamison Project, in 1987.

Since 1989, she has served as artistic director of the Alvin Ailey American Dance Theater. In 1993, Jamison wrote *Dancing Spirit: An Autobiography*.

BEVERLY JOHNSON

Beverly Johnson in 1975.

As the first black model to appear on the cover of *Vogue* magazine, Beverly Johnson, who was born in 1951 in Buffalo, New York, helped to change the fashion world's standard of "beauty."

Johnson earned a full academic scholarship to Northwestern University, but left after her freshman year to pursue a career in modeling. Within two years of moving to New York City, she had achieved supermodel status, appearing frequently on the covers of top fashion magazines, including *Glamour* and *Mademoiselle*. In 1974, she adorned the cover of the August issue of *Vogue*, breaking color barriers in a world where the popular image had always been "thin, white and blonde." And in 1975, Johnson was named Outstanding U.S. model.

Johnson continued modeling into the 1990s, dispelling the myth that a model's career is over after 10 years. She has appeared in films and music videos, and has written books of beauty tips specifically for African-American women.

JACK JOHNSON

Jack Johnson became the first black heavyweight champion when he defeated Tommy Burns in Sydney, Australia on December 26, 1908.

Born in Galveston, Texas in 1878, Johnson was so small as a child that he earned the nickname "Li'l Arthur," a name that stuck with him throughout his career. He learned boxing as a young adult, making his way around the country, working out with professional fighters when the opportunity presented itself. After his victory over Burns, Johnson became the center of a bitter racial controversy, as the American public showed their loyalty to the former white champion, Jim Jeffries. When Jeffries emerged from retirement to fight Johnson on July 14, 1910, he was knocked out in the 14th round.

Johnson lost the heavyweight crown in 1915 in a bout with Jess Willard, when he was knocked out in the twenty-sixth round. His career record was 107 wins, 6 losses. In 1946, Johnson was killed in an automobile accident in North Carolina. He was inducted into the Boxing Hall of Fame in 1954.

JOHN H. JOHNSON

As the founder of Johnson Publishing Company, which produces *Ebony* and *Jet* among other magazines, John Harold Johnson had, by 1989, amassed a net worth estimated at more than $150 million.

Johnson was born in Arkansas in 1918, and raised by his mother who often had to rely on welfare to support her family. A hard worker and good student, Johnson attended both Northeastern University and the University of Chicago, but chose to leave college when black business executive Harry Pace, the president of Supreme Life Insurance Co, offered him a job. While editing the company newsletter at Supreme, Johnson became interested in the idea of producing a black general interest magazine. *Negro Digest*, Johnson's first magazine, premiered in 1942 and by the end of 1943 had grown to a monthly circulation of 50,000. His next magazine, *Ebony*, was launched in 1945, followed by *Jet* in 1951. That year the United States Junior Chamber of Commerce named Johnson one of ten outstanding men of the year.

Johnson has also achieved success with his upscale line of beauty products called Fashion Fair, specifically designed to meet the needs of black women. He had published a book, *Before the Mayflower: A History of the Negro in America 1919-1962*, owns several radio stations including WJAC-AM in Chicago, and launched another magazine, *EM: Ebony Man*, in 1985. The Magazine Publishers of American named Johnson Publisher of the Year in 1972, and in 1987 he was inducted into the Black Press Hall of Fame. Johnson is active in politics and serves as board of director for several organizations, including Twentieth Century Fox. In 1989, Johnson's autobiography, *Succeeding Against the Odds,* was published.

EARVIN "MAGIC" JOHNSON

Earvin Johnson, Jr., earned the nickname "Magic" as a child, due to his amazing ball handling ability and skill on the basketball court. As a goodwill ambassador throughout his career, Magic has continually brought excitement and respect to the game of basketball.

Born in 1959 in Lansing, Michigan, Johnson was the sixth of ten children. His passion for basketball was evident from and early age. In high school Johnson made the all-state team all four years, leading his team to the state championship his senior year. He played college ball for two years, until he was drafted by the Los Angeles Lakers in 1979. During his first year with the Lakers, Johnson was chosen as the NBA Tournament MVP and named to the league's All Rookie Team. At six feet nine inches, he was the tallest guard in NBA history. That, combined with Johnson's brilliant playing and captivating personality, brought renewed life to his team and the attention of the media as well as prominent fans to their games. During the 1980's, Johnson led the Lakers to five NBA championships, and was named the league's MVP for three seasons.

In 1991, at the height of his career, Johnson shocked the public with the announcement that he had tested positive for HIV, forcing his retirement from the game. He has since become an active spokesperson for AIDS awareness, and created the Magic Johnson Foundation to raise funds for HIV and AIDS education, prevention and care. Johnson has made appearances on the court during his retirement, playing in the 1990 Olympics as well as in the 1992 NBA All-Star game, winning another MVP award. Johnson was chosen as one of the league's 50 all-time best players at the NBA's 50th anniversary celebration. Johnson now directs most of his energy toward several highly successful business ventures, all designed and located primarily to serve the black, urban community.

MORDECAI WYATT JOHNSON

Clergyman and educator Mordecai Wyatt Johnson was born in 1890 in Paris, Tennessee. He earned a succession of college degrees in English Literature, Social Sciences, and Theology at Morehouse College, University of Chicago and Rochester Theological Seminary between the years 1911 and 1916, while also serving as a professor at Morehouse. After earning an advanced degree in Theology from Harvard University, Johnson became a Baptist minister in West Virginia. In 1926, Johnson became the first African-American to be appointed president of Howard University, where he served for 34 years. At the time of his retirement, Howard was producing half the nation's black physicians and its law school was in the forefront of the civil rights movement. In 1929, Johnson was awarded the NAACP's Spingarn Medal for his outstanding contributions to the progress of African-Americans. Johnson died in 1976 in Washington, D.C.

FREDERICK McKINLEY JONES

Mechanic Frederick McKinely Jones, inventor of innovative products such as the first automatic refrigeration system for long haul trucks, was born in Cincinnati in 1892. He was raised by a priest after his mother died when he was a boy. He began as a mechanic's assistant, working his way up to chief mechanic on a Minnesota farm. After serving in World War II, his fame as a mechanic grew when he produced a series of devices to turn silent movie projectors into sound projectors.

The development of his truck refrigeration system, in 1935, brought about a change in the eating habits and patterns of the entire nation, as well as allowing for food production facilities to be developed at nearly any geographic location. Previously, food had been packed in ice, so that even a slight delay would result in spoilage.

In addition, Jones developed an air conditioning unit for military field hospitals, and a refrigerator for military field kitchens. In all, 61 patents were issued in Jones's name during his lifetime. He died in 1961.

JAMES EARL JONES

James Earl Jones, known for his booming voice and distinguished presence on stage and in film, broke a color barrier in Hollywood and on Broadway as one of the first black actors cast in roles traditionally undertaken by white actors. He has played lead roles in Shakespearean dramas, and was one of the first black regulars on a television soap opera in his role on *The Guiding Light*, in 1967.

Actor James Earl Jones shown here in 1995.

Jones, the son of actor Robert Earl Jones, was born in rural Mississippi in 1931. He was raised on his grandparents' farm in Michigan, studied drama at the University of Michigan and graduated cum laude in 1953. Jones made his Broadway debut in 1957 in *Wedding in June*, and went on to play a variety of notable stage roles during the early 1960s. It was his performance as Jack Jefferson, in the 1968 Broadway production, *The Great White Hope*, that brought Jones to prominence. He won a Tony award for the part, and was nominated for a Best Actor Oscar in 1970 for the film version.

He has been in many movies since, including *Coming to America*, *Hunt for Red October*, *Patriot Games*, and *Clear and Present Danger*. His distinctive voice brings life to many animated and unseen characters, most notably Darth Vader in the enormously successful *Star Wars* films. In 1985, Jones won his second Tony Award for his role in August Wilson's Pulitzer Prize winning drama *Fences*. He was inducted into the Theatre Hall of Fame the same year.

QUINCY JONES

As one of the most successful African-Americans in the history of popular music, Quincy Jones—musician, composer, arranger, producer and entertainment executive—has earned more than 70 Grammy Award nominations, won more than 25 Grammy Awards, as well as a Grammy Legends Award in 1991.

Jones was born in Chicago in 1933 and raised in Seattle, Washington. He studied trumpet as a child, and began playing professionally as a teenager in a band he formed with Ray Charles. At 16, Jones moved to Boston to attend the Berklee School of Music on a full scholarship. During the early 1950s, Jones became a regular member of Lionel Hampton's band, touring the U.S. and Europe.

He began recording jazz albums under his own name in the mid-1950s, and in 1961 was appointed musical director at Mercury Records. His promotion to vice president two years later made him the first African American to hold a senior executive position at a major record label. Jones left Mercury in 1965 and moved to Los Angeles to work full time on motion picture and television scores. He has composed the music for more than 30 films and shows, including *The Wiz* (1978) and *The Color Purple* (1985).

As an arranger and producer, Jones has worked with hundreds of performers and is probably best known for producing the album *Thriller* (1982), by Michael Jackson, and the song "We Are the World" (1985). As an entrepreneur, he founded his own record company, Qwest Records, in 1980. In 1993, Jones began publishing *Vibe* magazine, a joint venture with Time Warner, Inc. A year later he formed Qwest Broadcasting, with television stations in Atlanta and New Orleans. Jones has won Emmy Awards and Academy Awards for his musical scores, and numerous honorary degrees. He was featured in the 1991 documentary film, *Listen Up: The Lives of Quincy Jones*.

SCOTT JOPLIN

One of the most important developers of ragtime music, Scott Joplin combined the influences of classical music and the harmonies of African-American music, creating a unique individual style attempted by few other composers.

Joplin was born in 1868 near Texarkana, Texas. His father was a former slave, and although the family was poor, his mother saw to it that Joplin studied classical piano as a child. In his late teens, he became an itinerant piano player, traveling throughout the Midwest. After studying at the George R. Smith College for Negroes in Missouri, Joplin published his first commercially successful piano composition, "Maple Leaf Rag," in 1899. It became the most popular piano rag of the period.

In 1907, Joplin moved to New York City, where he published some 60 compositions including "The Entertainer," "The Cascades," the "Felicity Rag" and in 1901, the "Palm Leaf Rag." His 1911 ragtime opera, "Treemonisha," was one of the first indigenous black American operas. When "Treemonisha" failed in concert form in 1915 Joplin suffered a nervous breakdown, from which he never fully recovered. He died in a mental institution in 1917, from complications connected with tertiary syphilis.

Although he was almost forgotten at the time of his death, his ragtime compositions enjoyed a great revival in the 1970s, when his music was used as the background in the film *The Sting*. The Houston Grand Opera staged "Treemonisha" with enormous success in 1975. Altogether Joplin published 60 compositions, 41 of which are piano "rags."

BARBARA JORDAN

Barbara Jordan is a woman of firsts: the first African American since 1883 to be elected to the Texas State Senate, and the first woman ever to hold the position; the first black woman in the United States to preside over a legislative body as senate president *pro tempore* in Texas; the first black woman from a southern state to serve in Congress; and the first black keynote speaker at a Democratic national convention.

Barbara Jordan speaking at the Democratic National Convention in July, 1992.

Jordan was born in Houston, Texas, in 1936. She made the decision to become a lawyer in 10th grade while she attended Phillis Wheatley High School. After graduating magna cum laude from Texas State University, Jordan enrolled in Boston University Law School, where she was the only woman in a class of 128. In 1960, Jordan entered politics as a volunteer for John F. Kennedy's presidential campaign. In 1962, Jordan embarked on her own campaign for a seat in the Texas House of Representatives. Although she lost that race, she ran again in 1966 and won a seat in the state senate.

In 1968, Jordan was a delegate at the Democratic national convention, where her political stands worked to gain the support of President Lyndon B. Johnson. When Jordan waged a bid for a Congressional seat in 1972, she won 80 percent of the primary vote, and won the election by a margin of more than four to one. After her victory, she was appointed to the House Judiciary Committee.

Jordan became a national figure during the 1974 Watergate hearings and impeachment proceedings for President Richard Nixon. After speaking to Congress as a member of the House Judiciary Committee in favor of impeachment, *Newsweek* magazine called her speech "the most memorable indictment of Richard Nixon to emerge from the House impeachment." After serving her term, Jordan decided against running for re-election in 1978, and retired to a teaching position at the Lyndon B. Johnson School of Public Affairs at University of Texas. In 1988, Jordan was diagnosed with multiple sclerosis, but continued to teach despite being confined to a wheelchair. Although she had been out of the political arena for 15 years, in 1994 President Clinton named Jordan chairwoman of a task force to address the issue of illegal immigration. Because of her contributions she was awarded the Presidential Medal of Freedom in 1995.

On January 17, 1996, Jordan died of viral pneumonia at the age of 59. She is the first and only black woman to be buried in the Texas State Cemetery.

VERNON JORDAN

Attorney and civil rights leader Vernon Jordan has been as influential in the NAACP and Urban League, as he has been in corporate boardrooms and the highest councils of the U.S. government.

Jordan was born in Atlanta, Georgia in 1935 the second of three sons to Vernon, Sr., a postal clerk, and Mary, a successful caterer. He enrolled in DePaw University after graduating with honors from high school, and from there went on to Howard University Law School. In 1960 he became a

MICHAEL JORDAN

A sports phenomenon who has single-handedly turned professional basketball into an international spectator sport, Michael Jordan was born in Brooklyn, New York, in 1963, the fourth of five children. His family moved from New York to Wilmington, North Carolina when Michael was still a young child. As a young boy and teenager, Jordan showed more aptitude for baseball than basketball.

At Wilmington's Laney High School, Jordan didn't make the Varsity basketball team until his senior year. By then he was six feet three inches tall, and was recruited by University of North Carolina's coach Dean Smith. In 1981, Jordan became only the fourth freshman to earn a starting spot on the Tar Heels basketball team under coach Smith. During the 1982 NCAA championship game against Georgetown, Jordan was thrust into the national spotlight when he scored a last second jump-shot that sealed the Tar Heels victory by one point and earned the team the championship. The following year he was named All-American, and was chosen by *Sporting News* magazine as the college basketball player of the year. Jordan earned both honors again in 1984, and also won a gold medal at the Los Angeles Olympics as a member of the U.S. national team.

When the Chicago Bulls chose Jordan as the third pick in the NBA draft in 1984, Jordan decided to leave college after his junior year and signed a lucrative, five-year contract. His presence on the team immediately resurrected interest in the Chicago franchise, which had floundered in the early '80s. Leading the team in points, rebounds, assists and steals per game, Jordan was chosen Rookie of the Year in the NBA and earned a spot on the All-Star and All-Rookie teams. He became an NBA superstar when he won the slam-dunk contest during the 1988 All-Star game, after which he was given lucrative deals to endorse Nike sneakers and other products.

Jordan finally achieved his long-time goal of winning the league championship in 1991, leading his team to the NBA crown with an average of 31 points per game during the playoffs. With Jordan leading the team, the Bulls won the championship again the following two years, becoming the first team in more than 30 years to win three straight titles.

Tragedy struck in the summer of 1993 when Jordan's father was murdered, and Jordan shocked the world by announcing his retirement from basketball. After three consecutive NBA championships, Jordan stated he had "nothing left to prove." In 1994, he signed a contract to play baseball with the Chicago White Sox organization.

After playing in the minor leagues for two seasons, Jordan quit baseball in the spring of 1995, when the major league players went on strike. He ended his retirement from basketball just in time to rejoin the faltering Chicago Bulls for the 1995 season playoffs. The following season, Jordan once again led his team

Michael Jordan, shown here in Chicago, 1993.

to an NBA championship, the fourth for the Bulls, as well as the best regular-season record in history. Jordan and the Bulls went on to win the 1996-97 and the 1997-98 championships, earning the league Finals MVP award twice.

In addition to his extraordinary success on the court, Jordan has been especially influential in the sportswear industry. In 1984 Nike introduced their famous line of Air Jordan basketball shoes. Due to the successful partnership with Jordan, Nike has created a separate business unit known as the JORDAN brand, marketing footwear and clothing that Jordan himself helps design.

During his sports and business careers, Jordan has always dedicated himself to community interests. His annual celebrity golf tournament benefits a number of charities, and Jordan has maintained a long-time relationship with the Boys and Girls Club of Chicago.

clerk for a prominent attorney in Georgia who was leading the fight to end segregation in Georgia's colleges. The Georgia branch of the NAACP named Jordan field director in 1961, a post he remained in for two years, coordinating several civil rights campaigns.

Jordan moved to Arkansas in 1964 to head the Southern Regional Council's Voter Education Project. He remained with the project for four years. In 1970, he became executive director of the United Negro College Fund. Within a single year, he raised more than $10 million for the organization.

After only one year at the UNCF, Jordan was appointed director of the National Urban League, following the untimely death of director Whitney Young. Jordan's ease in dealing with the high-end establishment, combined with his effective people skills helped him obtain generous business and government funding for the Urban League. Jordan was able to procure connections for the League with prominent corporations after being appointed to the boards of Xerox, Bankers Trust, Dow Jones, and RJR Nabisco.

In the spring of 1990, after dining out with an Urban League volunteer in Indiana, Jordan was shot in the back by a sniper. He spent three months recuperating, and resigned from the League a year later, returning to his private law practice. With the election of Bill Clinton to the presidency in 1992, Jordan returned to the national spotlight, as one of the President's most trusted advisors. Although offered a number of posts in Clinton's administration, Jordan has chosen to aid the President in an unofficial capacity.

FLORENCE GRIFFITH JOYNER

Florence Griffith Joyner was the first female athlete to win four medals at one Olympic Games, with her record setting track performance at the 1988 Games in Seoul, South Korea. "Flojo's" combination of athletic prowess and glamour made her a media sensation.

Delorez Florence Griffith was born in 1959 in Los Angeles, one of eleven children. She began running track at the age of 7, and at 14 won the Jesse Owens National Youth Games. While at UCLA in the early 1980s, Griffith won national championships in the 200-meter and 400-meter dashes. She went on to win the silver medal in the 200-meter at the 1984 Olympic Games in Los Angeles. In 1987, she married Al Joyner—a champion jumper at the 1984 Games—and continued training for the 1988 Olympics, setting a world record at the trials in the 100-meter dash with a time of 10.49. At the summer Games in Seoul, she took gold medals in the 100-meter race, 200-meter race, and 4 x 100-meter relay, as well as a silver medal in the 4 x 400

relay. Her Olympic time of 21.34 in the 200-meter dash set a world record that still stands today.

In September 1998, Joyner's sudden death from a seizure related to epilepsy at her home in Mission Viejo, California, shocked the sporting world.

JACKIE JOYNER-KERSEE

A major force in track and field for more than 15 years, Jackie Joyner-Kersee, Flo Jo's sister-in-law, won the all-around heptathlon at the Olympic Games in 1988 and 1992, and garnered 6 Olympic medals overall.

Jacqueline Joyner was born in East St. Louis, Illinois. She began showing an aptitude for track as a young girl, and by the age of 12 was long jumping more than 17 feet. In 1976, at the age of 14, she won four consecutive junior national titles in the pentathlon. After graduating from high school in the top 10 percent of her class, she enrolled in UCLA on a basketball scholarship. Not only did she start on the basketball team all four years of college, she also won the NCAA hepatathlon in 1982 and 1983, as well as the silver medal in the heptathlon at the 1984 Olympics in Los Angeles. In 1986 she married her basketball coach, Bob Kersee, and gave up basketball to concentrate on the heptathlon, setting two world records in one month. At the Goodwill games in Moscow in 1986, Joyner-Kersee became the first woman in history to surpass the 7,000-point mark in the heptathlon.

At the 1987 World Track and Field championship in Rome, Joyner-Kersee became the first woman in history to win both a multi-sport event and an individual event at a major meet, when she won both the long jump and the heptathlon. The following year she took the gold medal in the heptathlon at the 1988 Olympics Games in Seoul, South Korea, setting a world record with her total points of 7,291. She also came home with the gold medal in the long jump.

At the 1992 Olympics in Barcelona she repeated her title in the heptathlon, and captured the bronze medal in the long jump.

In 1996, Joyner-Kersee competed in her fourth Olympics at the Atlanta Games. Although an injured hamstring forced her to drop out of the heptathlon after only one event, she managed to place third in the long jump, winning her sixth Olympic medal. Following the 1996 Olympics, Joyner-Kersee announced her retirement and has since formed her own company, Elite Sports Marketing. She has also created the Jackie Joyner-Kersee Community Foundation in East St. Louis to help needy children in her hometown. In 1998 she became the first woman chosen Athlete of the Year by *Sporting News*.

B. B. KING

After the release of his hit single "The Thrill is Gone," in 1969, for which he won the first of 9 Grammy Awards, blues artist B.B. King became an international success, influencing a whole generation of young musicians, including the Rolling Stones.

B.B. King in a Chicago concert in 1980.

Riley B. King was born in 1925, in Mississippi, the son of sharecroppers. He was first exposed to the blues by an aunt who played the music on a phonograph. King purchased his first guitar with money he had earned working in the cotton fields, and hitchhiked to Memphis, Tennessee, at the age of nineteen to perform in a club. He soon found a spot on a newly opened radio station, WDIA, where he would play for a few minutes each afternoon, and went on to become a disc jockey. First called "The Boy From Beale Street," then Blues Boy King, he thereafter became known as B.B. King.

King's first record was made in 1949, and he was a star in the rhythm and blues circuit with the release of "Three O'Clock Blues," "Sweet Black Angel," and "Rock Me Baby." "The Thrill is Gone" moved him into the national limelight. He now averages approximately 250 perfor-

mances a year, and has opened two jazz clubs, in Memphis and Universal City, California.

In partnership with lawyer F. Lee Bailey, King formed the Foundation for the Advancement of Inmate Recreation and Rehabilitation. He has received many honors which include an honorary doctorate from Yale University (1977), induction into the Rock and Roll Hall of Fame (1987), the Lifetime Achievement Award from the National Academy of Recording Arts and Sciences (1987), and the Presidential Medal of the Arts (1990). The NARAS Lifetime Achievement Award summed up King's accomplishments by stating that King is "one of the most original and soulful of all blues guitarists and singers, whose compelling style and devotion to musical truth have inspired so many budding performers, both here and abroad, to celebrate the blues." In 1995, King was a recipient of the Kennedy Center Honors.

CORETTA SCOTT KING

Coretta Scott King has become a major figure in the struggle for civil rights, carrying on the legacy of her husband, Dr. Martin Luther King, Jr.

Born in 1927, King is a native of Heilberger, Alabama. After graduating from high school in 1945, she received a scholarship to Antioch College, in Ohio, with a major in education and music. After graduating, she continued her music studies at the New England Conservatory of Music in Boston. It was while working to supplement her tuition in Boston that she met Martin Luther King, Jr., a student at Boston University. The couple married and moved back to Alabama in 1954, when Dr. King accepted a position as pastor of the Dexter Avenue Baptist Church in Montgomery.

During the early years of their marriage, King dedicated most of her time to raising their four children, while her husband engaged in his civil rights activities. Over the years, King gradually became more involved in her husband's work, occasionally performing at his lectures, leading the audiences in song. She used her musical training to develop a format for a freedom concert, incorporating hymns and spirituals in addition to freedom songs that narrated the civil rights struggle.

After the assassination of Martin Luther King, Jr. on April 4, 1968, King became much more involved in civil rights work. Her speech in Washington, D.C. on Solidarity Day, June 16, 1968, moved her into the spotlight, and the same year, she became the first woman commencement speaker at Harvard University.

In 1969, King began working on plans for the creation of

MARTIN LUTHER KING

Nobel Peace Prize winner Martin Luther King, Jr., was one of the principal leaders of the American civil rights movement and a leading advocate of non-violent protest.

King was born in Atlanta, Georgia in 1929, the eldest son of Martin Luther King, Sr., a Baptist minister, and Alberta King. King attended segregated public schools, including Booker T. Washington High School, the first black public high school in Atlanta. He entered Morehouse College in Atlanta at the age of 15. After graduating with a bachelor's degree in 1948, he entered Crozer Theological Seminary in Pennsylvania, and from there went on to Boston University, where he earned a doctoral degree in theology in 1955.

In 1953, he met and married Coretta Scott. They moved to Montgomery, Alabama, when King accepted his first pastorate at the Dexter Avenue Baptist Church in 1954.

On December 1, 1955, Rosa Parks, a leading member of the Montgomery branch of the NAACP, was ordered to relinquish her seat on a bus to a white passenger. When she refused and was jailed, local NAACP leaders chose King to be president of the Montgomery Improvement Association (MIA), the organization that directed the Montgomery Bus Boycott. The boycott lasted a year, and resulted in ending the "whites only" sections of Montgomery buses—and ultimately all public transportation in the country.

The boycott brought King, only in his twenties, national attention as one of the most powerful leaders of the civil rights movement, but also put him in danger. In 1956, his home was bombed.

King's next accomplishment was to help found the Southern Leadership Conference (SCLC) in 1957, an organization of black churches and ministers who challenged racial segregation. King and other SCLC leaders encouraged the use of non-violent action to protest discrimination, including marches, demonstrations and boycotts.

In the early 1960s, King's SCLC protest campaigns gained national attention. His 1963 anti-segregation marches and demonstrations in Birmingham, Alabama, resulted in an end to some forms of segregation in Birmingham, as well as encouraging Americans nationwide to support legislation against segregation. During the demonstrations, King was arrested and jailed. King's "Letter from Birmingham City Jail," written to local clergymen who had criticized him, argued that individuals had the moral right and responsibility to dis-obey unjust laws. The letter was widely read and added to King's standing as a moral leader.

The success of the Birmingham efforts led other black leaders to help King organize the 1963 March on Washington. On August 28, King delivered his famous "I have a dream . . ." speech to an audience of more than 200,000 civil rights' supporters gathered in front of the Lincoln Memorial. The speech and the march, together with King's earlier public efforts on behalf of civil rights, resulted in the Civil Rights Act of 1964, which prohibited segregation in public accommodations, as well as discrimination in education and employment. For his effectiveness as a leader of the Civil Rights movement and his highly visible morality, King was awarded the 1964 Nobel Prize for peace, the youngest recipient ever.

In 1965, the SCLC helped lead a voting rights march from Selma, Alabama, to the state capitol in Montgomery. The march contributed to the passage of the Voting Rights Act of 1965, which guaranteed African Americans access to political participation.

King began to focus his civil rights activism on economic issues, and in 1967 and 1968 he began to organize the Poor People's March on Washington. While making a stop in Memphis to address local striking sanitation workers, on April 4th, 1968, King was assassinated by a sniper later identified at James Earl Ray. King's death at the age of 39 prompted rioting in more than 100 U.S. cities. King has come to represent black courage and achievement, high moral leadership, and the ability of Americans to recognize and try to overcome racial differences.

a Martin Luther King, Jr. Memorial in Atlanta, which is now part of the National Park Service. King also established the Martin Luther King, Jr. Center for Social Change in Atlanta, which awards an annual prize to a practitioner of non-violent efforts to further peace and civil rights. In 1983, she won the Franklin D. Roosevelt Freedom Medal for epitomizing his four freedoms—worship, speech, from want, and from fear. King, along with two other famous civil rights widows–Betty Shabazz and Myrlie Evers-Williams—were honored for their influence by the National Political Congress of Black Women in 1995.

EARTHA KITT

Actress and singer Eartha Kitt, born in South Carolina in 1925, grew up working in the cotton fields with her family. As a child she was sent to New York to live with her aunt. After dropping out of high school she worked as a seamstress, then joined the Katherine Dunham Dance Troupe, traveling throughout Europe and Mexico. When Kitt returned to the U.S. and became a featured entertainer in the revue, New Faces of 1952, she drew rave reviews. She went on to star in the drama *Mrs. Patterson* (1954), and by the end of the 1950s was performing regularly in other stage productions.

As a recording artist, Kitt reached an even broader audience with her hits "C'est Si Bon" (1953) and "Santa Baby" (1953). She made frequent guest appearances on television variety shows and had a regular role as "Catwoman" in the 1967 series *Batman*. Her film credits include *St. Louis Blues* (1958), and the title role in *Anna Lucasta* (1959).

Known for being outspoken on political and social issues, Kitt experienced a drastic reduction in work opportunities for nearly ten years, after publicly criticizing President Lyndon Johnson during a White House luncheon hosted by Lady Bird Johnson in the 1960s. Kitt returned to the stage triumphantly in *Timbuktu*, a 1978 adaptation of Geoffrey Holder's *Kismet*, in which Kitt had the starring role. She now performs her night club act worldwide.

GLADYS KNIGHT

In 1988, at the second annual Soul Train Music Awards, Gladys Knight & the Pips celebrated 30 years of recording by receiving the Heritage Award. Gladys Knight's singing career began at the age of eight, when she won a $2,000 first prize on the television show *Ted Mack's Amateur Hour* for her rendition of the song "Too Young."

Born in Atlanta, Georgia in 1944, Knight joined forces with her brother, Merald and sister Brenda, as well as two of their cousins to form a vocal group. They performed gospel at a local church until 1957, when another cousin, James "Pips" Woods suggested they turn professional and became their manager. They called themselves the Pips in his honor. After recording for several different record labels, and surviving various personnel changes within the group, the Pips, consisting of Knight, brother Merald, cousin William Guest, Langston George, and Edward Patten, signed with the Motown subsidiary, Soul.

In 1967, the group released the single "I Heard It Through the Grapevine," which reached number two on the *Billboard* charts. The song was nominated for a Grammy, eventually selling over a million copies. Other hits included "Take Me in Your Arms and Love Me," "The End Of Our Road," "Nitty Gritty," "Friendship Train," "I Don't Want To Do Wrong" and "If I Were Your Woman," which was nominated for a Grammy Award in 1970. After seven years at Motown, the group decided to move on, but left on a positive note with their big hit "Neither One of Us (Wants To Be The First To Say Goodbye)." Not only did this song reach #2 in the U.S. and sell over a million copies, it also won the group the 1973 Grammy for Best Pop Vocal Performance by a Duo, Group or Chorus.

After leaving Motown, the group remained successful, signing first with Buddha and later with CBS and MCA Records. Joined by Dionne Warwick and Elton John, Knight recorded the Grammy winning gold single, "That's What Friends Are For" in 1986. The group parted ways in 1989, reuniting briefly the following year to perform on the television special "Motown 30: What's Goin' On!" In 1996 they were inducted into the Rock and Roll Hall of Fame.

LEWIS LATIMER

Lewis H. Latimer, a pioneer in the development of the electric light bulb, was the only African American member of Thomas A. Edison's research team of noted scientists. Born in Massachusetts in 1848, Latimer used the skills he learned in mechanical drawing while in the Navy to land him a job as a draftsman with a firm of patent solicitors. He began working on his own inventions, and in 1874 had his first patent approved for a "water closet for railway cars." From there, Latimer went to work at United States Electric Lighting Company, where he developed and patented the process for manufacturing carbon filaments for incandescent light bulbs.

In 1896 Latimer became chief draftsman and expert witness to the Board of Patent Control of the company that eventually became known as General Electric. Latimer became a patent consultant for the engineer and patent lawyer Edwin Hammer in 1911. He continued with his inventions and teaching drafting skills until his death in 1928.

SPIKE LEE

Controversial filmmaker Spike Lee rose from obscurity to fame with the release of his 1986 low-budget, independent feature film *She's Gotta Have It*.

Born Shelton Jackson Lee in Atlanta, Georgia in 1957, Lee grew up in Brooklyn, New York. After attending Morehouse College, he did his graduate work in film at New York University, where his senior thesis film, *Joe's Bed-Stuy Barbershop: We Cut Heads* (1982), won a student Academy Award and was showcased at Lincoln Center and at the Museum of Modern Art.

After the critical and financial success of *She's Gotta Have It*, Lee released three more films in as many years, all depicting realistic views of African American life: *School Daze* (1988), *Do the Right Thing* (1989), and *Mo' Better Blues* (1990). Lee told *Ebony* magazine in 1989 that his intention is "to present racism and other problems so that discussions can start and solutions can be found."

In 1991, Lee released *Jungle Fever*, a film about interracial love affairs, followed by *Malcolm X* (1992), the story of the slain black leader's life. Since then, Lee has released several films including *Crooklyn* (1994), *Clockers* (1995), *Girl 6* (1996), *Get On the Bus* (1996), *He Got Game* (1998), and most recently *Summer of Sam* (1999). In his Brooklyn neighborhood, Lee established his own production company —40 Acres and a Mule—and on each of his films, he has provided hundreds of jobs for actors, designers, stagehands, lighting specialists and other technicians from the black community. Lee has founded a minority scholarship fund at New York University's film school and supports a number of charities, including the United Negro College Fund.

CARL LEWIS

In 1984, track and field star Carl Lewis became the first athlete, since Jesse Owens in 1936, to win four gold medals in Olympic competition. He set Olympic records in

Carl Lewis, setting World's Record 100-meter in 1991.

two of the gold medal events, the 200-meter dash, and the 400-meter relay.

Frederick Carlton Lewis was born in Birmingham, Alabama and educated at the University of Houston. He qualified for the 1980 Olympic Games in Moscow, but was unable to compete due to the U.S. boycott of the Games. After winning world championships in the 100-meter dash and long jump in 1983, he again qualified for the 1984 Olympics in Los Angeles, where he enjoyed his greatest performance, earning gold medals in the 100 and 200-meter dashes, the long jump, and the 4 x 100-meter relay.

At the 1987 World Championships in Rome, Italy, Lewis was beaten in the 100-meter dash by Canadian Ben Johnson. He again lost to Johnson in the 100-meter dash at the 1988 Olympic Games in Seoul, South Korea, but when Johnson was disqualified from competition for using banned substances, Lewis was declared the winner. At the same time, he was retroactively declared the winner of the 1987 World Championships. In Seoul, Lewis also won the gold medal in the long jump and placed second in the 200-meter dash.

At the 1992 Olympics in Barcelona, Spain, Lewis won two more gold medals in the 4 x 100-meter relay and the long jump. In 1996 he won his fourth straight Olympic gold medal in the long jump at the Games in Atlanta, Georgia. His victory made him only the fourth man ever to win nine gold medals at the summer Games. Lewis set numerous world records in his events during his career, and was inducted into the Olympic Hall of Fame in 1985. He retired from competition in 1997.

REGINALD LEWIS

Business executive Reginald Lewis was born in Baltimore in 1942. After graduating from Virginia State College in 1965, he went on to Harvard Law School where he received his degree in 1968. Upon graduating he began working as an attorney in various law firms, and in 1970 became a partner in the first African American law firm on Wall Street, Murphy, Thorpe and Lewis. Between 1973 and 1989, Lewis worked in private practice as a corporate lawyer, and in 1989 joined TLC Beatrice Holdings Inc. as president and CEO. When TLC acquired Beatrice International Food Co., Lewis became the head of the largest African-American owned business in the United States.

Lewis served on the board of directors for several organizations, was a member of the American and National Bar Associations, and the National Conference of Black Lawyers. In 1974 he was presented with the Distinguished Service Award by the American Association of MESBIC, and the Black Enterprise Achievement Award for the Professions. Lewis died unexpectedly in 1993 in New York.

JOE LOUIS

Joe Louis in Kansas City, Missouri.

Widely respected by Americans of all color, the man known as the "Brown Bomber" dominated the world of boxing for eleven years, holding the heavyweight title from June 1937 until June of 1948.

Joseph Louis Barrow was born in Lafayette, Alabama on May 13, 1914. The family moved to Detroit when Louis was a child, where they lived in dire poverty. After dropping out of school in the fifth grade, Louis took up boxing at a local recreation center. He began to take boxing seriously while working at an auto plant at the age of 18.

During his first two years as an amateur, Louis knocked out 43 of 45 opponents. He turned professional after capturing the national light-heavyweight championship crown in 1934. In June of 1937, Louis became the first African American to win the heavyweight title since Jack Johnson, when he knocked out American boxer James Jack Braddock in the eighth round. Over a span of 12 years, Louis successfully defended his title 25 times. His first, and most devastating, loss came in 1936 to the German boxer Max Schmeling. The Nazis equated Schmeling's victory over Louis to a validation of Nazi superiority over democracy, and the "master race's" superiority over blacks. Louis became a national hero and a symbol of freedom when he faced Schmeling in a rematch in 1938, scoring a devastating first-round knockout. The fight is considered to be one of the greatest moments in boxing history.

During his professional career, Louis compiled 68 victories and 3 defeats, with 54 knockouts. He retired from boxing in 1949, returning to the ring briefly, but unsuccessfully, to the ring in 1950, after which he retired permanently. In 1954, Louis was elected to the Boxing Hall of Fame. Louis died in 1981.

WYNTON MARSALIS

Trumpet player Wynton Marsalis, the first jazz artist to win the Pulitzer Prize for music, is known for his ability to play jazz and classical music with equal facility, becoming the first musician to win Grammy Awards in both categories in the same year.

Marsalis was born in New Orleans, Louisiana in 1961. His father, Ellis Marsalis, was a professional jazz musician and teacher, who strongly influenced his son's early musical development. Wynton began taking trumpet lessons at age 12, and went on to the attend the Berkshire Music Center in Massachusetts, and the Julliard School of Music in New York City. At age 19 he toured with Art Blakey's Jazz Messengers band and a year later joined Herbie Hancock's jazz quartet for an extended tour and a number of recording sessions.

In 1981, his debut jazz album, *Wynton Marsalis*, was released, followed in 1983 by *Trumpet Concertos*, his classical recording debut. The same year, Marsalis formed his own jazz quintet, which included his brother Branford on saxophone, and the group released its first album, *Think One*.

Marsalis expanded his group to a septet, and began to focus his attention on nurturing young talent. He used his popularity and prestige to organize jazz performances and special tributes to long-established jazz artists. In 1987, Marsalis co-founded Jazz at Lincoln Center, a concert series that brought together some of the biggest names in jazz. His 1989 and 1991 recordings, *Majesty of the Blues*, and the trilogy *Soul Gestures in Southern Blue* represented a return to his New Orleans jazz and blues roots with a contemporary sound.

Marsalis disbanded his jazz septet at the end of 1994 to concentrate on leading the Lincoln Center Jazz Orchestra. He expanded his range as a composer, writing a number of ballet scores for major companies including *Griot New York*, *Jazz: Six Syncopated Movements*, and *Jump Start*. His most notable jazz compositions include *Blue Interlude, In This House, On This Morning* and *Blood on the Fields*, which won him the Pulitzer Prize in 1997. Marsalis has written many scores for television and film, and earned several Grammy Awards. He has authored the books *Sweet Swing Blues on the Road* (1994), and *Marsalis on Music* (1995). Since 1995, Marsalis has hosted an educational series on National Public Radio, *Making the Music*. In 1998 Marsalis released the album *Midnight Blues–Standard Time*, on which he performs with a 31-piece orchestra.

THURGOOD MARSHALL

Civil rights lawyer Thurgood Marshall argued many groundbreaking cases in local, state and federal courts as well as the Supreme Court, before becoming the first African-American Justice on the Supreme Court of the United States.

Supreme Court Justice Marshall in 1990.

Born Thoroughgood Marshall in Baltimore, Maryland in 1908, his name was shortened to Thurgood in second grade. After graduating from an all-black high school at the age of 16, Marshall enrolled in Pennsylvania's Lincoln University, the nation's oldest black college. He finished first in his class of 1933 at Howard University Law School.

After a short stint in private practice, Marshall moved to New York in 1936 to become a staff lawyer for the NAACP. From 1939 to 1961, he served as director and chief counsel for the NAACP Legal Defense and Education Fund, and won most of his cases in front of the Supreme Court. His most important victory was *Brown v. Board of Education of Topeka*, in 1954. In this case, Marshall persuaded the court to unanimously declare segregation in public schools unconstitutional. The decision was the precursor to the civil rights movement of the 1950s and 1960s, and put Marshall at the forefront of the movement. In the 1950s Marshall won six other Supreme Court cases which led to the desegregation of public parks, swimming pools, local bus systems and recreational facilities.

During the early 1960s, Marshall served on the United States Court of Appeals before becoming solicitor general of the United States. In 1967, President Lyndon Johnson appointed Marshall to the Supreme Court, where he was sworn in by a vote of 69–11.

Marshall was a prominent member of the court's liberal majority, strongly defending the right to freedom of speech, and opposing the death penalty. When the court became increasingly conservative during the 1980s, Marshall held to his liberal views and was often the lone dissenting voice. He voted in favor of protecting a women's right to safe, legal abortion, and was an advocate for the uneducated and poor.

Health problems and advancing age forced Marshall to step down from the Supreme Court in 1991, after a long and illustrious career. He died of heart failure in 1993 in Washington, D.C., and was buried in Arlington National Cemetery.

WILLIE MAYS

Baseball player Willie Mays, also known as the "Say Hey Kid," earned a reputation as a right-handed hitter with a distinctive style and great power. His defensive skills in centerfield caused Joe DiMaggio to say that Mays had the greatest throwing arm in baseball.

Mays was born in 1931 in Alabama. His father, Willie Mays, Sr., was a semi-professional baseball player who fostered his son's early interest in the sport. By his early teens, Mays was playing on his father's factory team alongside men twice his age.

In high school he was a star athlete in baseball, basketball and football. In 1948, at just seventeen years old, Mays left school to play baseball in the Negro American League with the Birmingham Black Barons. Within two years he was spotted by a scout for the New York Giants, and began playing for the organization's minor league team. By 1951, Mays was promoted to the majors.

Mays put his baseball career on hold for two years, to serve in the U.S. Army. Rejoining the Giants in 1954, he led

Willie Mays at bat for the New York Giants.

the team into the 1954 World Series, hitting forty-one home runs and leading the National League in hitting his first year back. His famous catch during the eighth inning of the first game of the Series is one of the most talked-about plays in baseball history. That year he was chosen for the National League's All-Star Team and was voted the league's Most Valuable Player. Mays was an exciting player to watch and quickly became a favorite of the fans. His "basket" catches, an underhand wrist-level catch of fly balls, became his trademark.

When the Giants moved to San Francisco in 1958, Mays continued to be among the league's leading players. He played for the Giants for 22 years, until he was traded to the New York Mets in 1972, where he played his last two seasons of baseball. His career statistics rank Mays among the top baseball players of all time. He was the first player to hit 300 home runs and steal 300 bases in a career, and the first National League player to hit 600 home runs. Mays finished with a total of 660 home runs and a lifetime batting average of .302. During his career he played in 24 All-Star games and won the Golden Glove award for defensive play 12 times. Mays was inducted into the Baseball Hall of Fame in 1979. In 1986 Mays returned to the Giants as a special assistant to the club president.

JAMES MEREDITH

Civil rights activist James Meredith gained notoriety when he became the first African-American student to enter the University of Mississippi in 1962. He has since become a controversial figure for not only challenging racism, but also for his conservative politics and questioning the tactics of established African-American rights groups.

Meredith was born in 1933 in Kosciusko, Mississippi, the seventh of thirteen children. After serving nine years in the U.S. Air Force, Meredith returned to his home state to fight what he considered a war against white supremacy. Meredith called upon the NAACP to help him file a lawsuit against the University of Mississippi for its discriminatory admissions policy excluding African-Americans. U.S. district court ruled against Meredith, but upon appeal the decision was overturned and found in his favor. Attempting to enter the University, Meredith was turned away three times by angry mobs threatening violence. When he finally enrolled successfully, rioting broke out on campus, two people were killed and many more wounded. Although he never led a "normal" student life, Meredith did graduate in the summer of 1963 with a degree in history and political science. His 1966 autobiography, *Three Years in Mississippi*, states that he felt a "divine responsibility" to defeat the system of white supremacy in Mississippi.

During his time at the University of Mississippi and since, James has often challenged the existing black political establishment. In 1989, he joined the staff of conservative North Carolina senator Jesse Helms, who had opposed civil rights legislation. Meredith's conservative views held that social programs such as welfare encouraged black dependence. Although he draws criticism from many in the black establishment, Meredith also garners high praise for his individuality and willingness to fight for his beliefs.

THELONIUS MONK

Jazz pianist Thelonius Monk's unique musical style as an instrumentalist and a composer made him a leader in the development of modern jazz.

Born in 1917 in North Carolina, Monk spent most of his childhood in New York City. After studying for a short time at the Julliard School, he was hired as a jazz pianist at Minton's nightclub and continued playing there during the years when a new type of jazz, known as bebop, and later just bop, began to emerge. During the 1940s, Monk was a notable figure on the jazz scene in New York City, although he did not receive full recognition for the contribution he made to the new jazz, or record to the extent of some of his jazz peers. It wasn't until the 1950s that Monk began to receive more attention and emerge as an influential figure in the jazz world. He formed his own jazz quartet, which lasted for most of the 1960s. When saxophonist John Coltrane joined the quartet, people began to recognize Monk as one of the great stars of jazz. Many of his tunes, such as "Round Midnight," "Epistropy," "Well, You Needn't," "Rhythm-a-ling," and "Straight, No Chaser" have become jazz standards. In 1962, Monk signed an extended contract with Columbia records, and two years later he was featured on the cover of *Time* magazine. Symphony orchestras perform his compositions, and other jazz musicians often use his musical creations in their own performances and recordings.

Monk's last recordings were made during a world tour in 1971, after which he stopped performing altogether. He died of a stroke in 1982 in Englewood, New Jersey.

TONI MORRISON

Toni Morrison's books dealing with the black experience and celebrating the black community have won numerous prizes over the years, including the Pulitzer, but her greatest literary achievement was to become the first African-American female author to be awarded the Nobel Prize in Literature in 1993.

Morrison was born Chloe Anthony Wofford in Lorain, Ohio in 1931. After graduating from high school she studied literature at Howard University, and from there went on to Cornell University where she earned her M.A. in English in 1955. Morrison became a college professor, teaching English at Texas Southern University and Howard University from 1955 to 1964. A few years later she moved to New York and began a career as an editor at Random House. At the same time, she taught literature classes in the New York State university system, Yale University and Bard College.

Morrison's first novel, *The Bluest Eye*, was published in 1970. Three years later she published *Sula*. Both novels focused on African American girls and women, the problems they face in the white world, and the intricacies of being female in the black community. The publication of her first two novels brought Morrison national recognition as a critic and scholar of literature and African-American culture.

In 1977, Morrison published *Song of Solomon* continuing her exploration of black heritage and culture. Her next work, *Tar Baby*, came out in 1981 and became an instant success, remaining on the *New York Times* bestseller list for four months. The book was again an exploration of the relationship between black and white culture, this time set in the U.S. and the Caribbean.

Toni Morrison at the Nobel Prize Awards in 1993.

Morrison's fifth novel was her 1987 Pulitzer Prize winning work, *Beloved*. *Beloved* is about the interior life of slavery, a tale of a woman who kills one of her children to save it from living in slavery. Morrison describes the book as "an effort to rescue the 'sixty million and more' to whom she dedicates it from the oblivion they had been consigned by history." Her sixth critically acclaimed novel, *Jazz*, was published in 1992. The same year, she published the non-fiction book *Playing in the Dark: Whiteness and the Literary Imagination*. The seventh novel by Morrison, *Paradise* (1998), focuses on an all-black town and a violent attack on a small community of women within the town.

After winning the Nobel Prize, Morrison was further honored by being named the Jefferson Lecturer in the Humanities by the National Endowment of the Humanities, in 1996.

JELLY ROLL MORTON

Jazz pianist Jelly Roll Morton, one of the earliest composers and piano players of jazz, performed a unique blend of blues, ragtime, Creole and Spanish music. He was an important transitional figure between ragtime and jazz piano styles. An eccentric and temperamental man, his important contributions to jazz have often been overshadowed by his colorful lifestyle.

Born Ferdinand Joseph LaMenthe in 1890, Morton was raised in the sophisticated Creole culture of New Orleans. As a child he studied classical piano with composer Tony Jackson. During his teens he began playing in the whorehouses and bordellos in the Storyville district of New Orleans. After traveling and working various jobs throughout the South and Midwest, Morton settled in Chicago in 1912 where he published his first composition, "Jelly Roll Blues." A talented arranger, he wrote special scores that took advantage of the three-minute limitation of 78 rpm records.

Morton hit his stride in 1922, and a year later began making records with the New Orleans Rhythm Kings. From 1926 to 1930, he toured and recorded with his own band, Red Hot Peppers. A pioneer of organizing players into a loose orchestra, Morton introduced a number of popular classics, including "King Porter Stomp" and "Mournful Serenade."

In the early 1930s, Morton moved to New York, where the popularity of early jazz had begun to be replaced by the new big-band sound of "swing." With his career in decline, he moved to Washington D.C. in 1935 and began working in small clubs. Morton died in 1941 in California.

EDWIN MOSES

Track star Edwin Moses was undefeated in his event, the 400-meter hurdles, for more than ten years, winning two Olympic gold medals during his decade of dominance.

Moses was born in Ohio in 1955, the son of teachers. During high school he ran track, and continued while attending Morehouse College on an academic scholarship. The summer he graduated from college he set an American record in the Olympic trials of 48.3 seconds for the 400-meter hurdles. At the Montreal Olympics in 1976, Moses continued to excel in his event, winning a gold medal in world-record time of 47.64 seconds.

After winning the World Cup 400-meter hurdles the following year, Moses began a string of 122 consecutive victories, defeating all opponents until June of 1987. He was unable to compete in the Moscow Olympics in 1980, due to the American boycott of the Games, but did take the gold medal at the Los Angeles games in 1984. In 1988 he won the bronze medal at the Olympics in Seoul, South Korea. During his reign as the top performer in the 400-meter hurdles, Moses became a spokesperson on behalf of track and field athletes, demanding better treatment and higher prize money for track competitors.

ELIJAH MUHAMMED

Nation of Islam leader Elijah Muhammed led the Black Muslims from 1934 until the time Malcolm X became a more visible spokesperson in the 1950s and 1960s. He preached separatism for blacks as the key to African-American advancement.

Elijah Muhammed was born Elijah Poole in Georgia in 1897, one of thirteen children of poor tenant farmers who were former slaves. After leaving Georgia at the age of 16, he settled in Detroit in 1923. During the depression he met and became a follower of Wallace Fard, the founder of the Nation of Islam. Under Fard's influence, Poole changed his name to Muhammed, and was appointed supreme minister of the Nation of Islam.

Under his leadership, the Muslim followers took on prohibitions against alcohol, narcotics, and gambling, and were disciplined if they lied, stole or were discourteous.

The strong ethics within the Nation of Islam community were in stark contrast to Muhammed's interpretation of the white community's immoral lifestyle. The collective "white man" was perceived as the devil and the incarnation of evil, the user of black people for the wealth of the white economy.

While white society perceived the Muslim antipathy toward it as a threat, many African-Americans were attracted by Muhammed's ideologies. By the late 1960s and early 1970s, Muhammed had moderated the Nation's criticism of whites without compromising its message of black integrity.

Elijah Muhammed died in Chicago in 1975. At the time of his death, the Nation of Islam was an important religious, political and economic force among America's blacks, particularly in the large, urban areas.

EDDIE MURPHY

Beginning with his box office smash hit, *48 Hours*, in 1982, actor/comedian Eddie Murphy turned out five movies in the 1980s that grossed over $100 million. His films have grossed a combined estimate of $2 billion worldwide, making Murphy one of the first African American box office stars to be successful the world over.

Edward Regan Murphy was born in April, 1961 in Brooklyn, New York. His parents were divorced when he was three years old, and at the age of 8, his father was killed. Within a year, his mother re-married and the family moved

Eddie Murphy in August 1987.

to Roosevelt, Long Island, where Eddie spent the rest of his childhood. As a child, Murphy entertained his friends and classmates with cartoon and celebrity imitations, and by 15 he was hosting talent shows at local clubs. The managers of New York's Comic Strip club saw him perform, and later became Murphy's personal managers.

Murphy continued performing at local clubs while attending Nassau Community College, until he auditioned for a part for the 1980-82 season of *Saturday Night Live* on television. He was hired as a supporting cast member, but after creating such roles as Mr. Robinson, Little Richard Simmons, Velvet Jones, Raheem Abdul Muhammed and Tyrone Green, eventually was given a lead role.

In 1982, Murphy got his big film break at the age of only 21, when he was cast in *48 Hours*, which became an instant box office smash. His successful performance in his first movie led to his role opposite Dan Ackroyd in *Trading Places* (1983), another huge hit. Murphy's third film, *Beverly Hills Cop* (1985), in which he had his first starring role, broke all previous box office records its opening weekend. The film went on to gross domestic receipts of more than $200 million. Now an established Hollywood superstar, Murphy was given one of the most lucrative contracts at the time by Paramount Pictures. Murphy finished the 1980s with *The Golden Child* (1986), *Beverly Hills Cop II* (1987), *Hollywood Shuffle* (1987), *Coming to America* (1988), and *Harlem Nights* (1989), which he wrote and directed. Murphy's stand-up film, *Raw* (1987), was the highest-grossing concert film ever, with receipts of over $50 million.

After experiencing a dip in his career in the early 1990s, Murphy made a comeback with the release of *The Nutty Professor* in the summer of 1996. The movie went on to gross over $100 million and proved that Murphy was still an enormous box-office draw. In addition, Murphy has released two record albums, and created Eddie Murphy Television enterprises. He received a Golden Globe award and the NAACP Image Award for his work in *Trading Places*; Emmy nominations for *Saturday Night Live*; a Grammy Award in 1984 for best comedy album, the NAACP Lifetime Achievement Award in 1991; his own star on the Hollywood Walk of Fame; and an *Essence* Magazine Spirit Award in 1994.

HUEY NEWTON

Founder and leader of the Black Panther party, Huey P. Newton was born in Louisiana in 1942, the youngest of seven children. The family moved to Oakland, California where Huey grew up and attended high school. After graduating, he enrolled in Oakland's Merrit College, earned an associate degree, and then spent a semester at San Francisco Law School. While he was studying law, Newton became active in community politics and became friends with fellow student activist Bobby Seale. Together they created the Black Panther Party in 1966, to take action on behalf of blacks against what was perceived as the white power structure, affirming the use of violence as a means of self-defense.

In 1967, Newton was arrested for killing an Oakland police officer during a dispute, although the actual events were unclear. In response, the Black Panthers began a "Free Huey" campaign that drew a national following. Newton pleaded not guilty, but was convicted of manslaughter. He was released from prison two years later when the conviction was overturned. Rejoining the Black Panthers, Newton sought to revive the party by focusing on community service and advocating nonviolent political action.

Despite his new attitude, Newton continued to run into trouble, and at one point fled to Cuba for three years to escape prosecution on various criminal charges. He returned to the U.S. in 1977, and resumed his education, earning a bachelor's degree and a PhD. from University of California, Santa Cruz in 1980. In August of 1989, Newton was found dead on an Oakland street, the victim of a shooting. The motive is said to have been drug related, but has never been fully established.

JESSYE NORMAN

Opera singer Jessye Norman was born in 1945 in Georgia and began singing in church when she was four years old. She studied voice and trained at Howard University, where she received her bachelor's degree, cum laude, in

1967. She went on to study at Peabody Conservatory and received her master's degree from University of Michigan in 1968. The same year, the gifted soprano won a voice competition in Munich, Germany, and in 1969 she made her operatic debut in Berlin in *Tannhauser*, by Robert Wagner.

In her early career, Norman sang in renowned opera houses throughout Europe, during which time much of her operatic repertoire was recorded. She returned to the U.S. in 1982 to perform in Philadelphia. The following year Norman debuted at New York's Metropolitan Opera House, performing as Cassandra in *Les Troyens*.

Jessye Norman in August 1989.

Norman's recital programs combine operatic arias and spirituals with art songs in various languages. Her repertory includes German, Austrian, Hungarian and French roles. She is adept at performing Wagner, and includes several of his heroines in her German repertory. Norman has received numerous awards for her work, including several Grammys, an Outstanding Musician of the Year Award, and several honorary degrees from American universities. In 1996, the Riverwalk Amphitheater and Plaza in Augusta, Georgia was dedicated and named for her. Jessye Norman lives in New York City, where she continues to perform when not touring worldwide.

ODETTA

In a performing career that has spanned forty years, folk singer/guitarist Odetta has played for audiences throughout the world in concert halls, clubs and universities; accompanied ballet companies and symphony orchestras and acted in large stage productions.

Odetta Holmes Felious Gordon was born in 1930 in Birmingham, Alabama. She began taking singing lessons at the age of thirteen, and developed and early love of classical music. Her original goal was to sing opera, but after being introduced to folk music while performing in *Finian's Rainbow* as a teenager, she became hooked. Odetta emerged on the folk scene in San Francisco in the early 1950s, playing a guitar, and over the years she has collaborated with other major folk stars, among them Pete Seeger, Joan Baez, Buffy St. Marie, and the late Elizabeth Cotton, and has toured Europe with vocal artists Miriam Makeba and Nina Simone. Her film credits include *Cinerama Holiday* (1955), and *Sanctuary* (1960).

The Federation of Protestant Charities and the World Folk Music Association honored Odetta with Lifetime Achievement Awards for her contributions to numerous humanitarian organizations and causes. She says her purpose is to be useful, performing "wherever and whenever I'm needed."

JOSEPH "KING" OLIVER

Cornetist Joseph "King" Oliver was one of the earliest major jazz figures, and mentor to trumpeter Louis Armstrong, who referred to him as "Papa Joe." Oliver is given credit for having developed the use of cups, glasses, mutes and buckets, as well as much of the phraseology that made up the vernacular of jazz's roots.

Joe Oliver was born in Louisiana in 1885, and initially played both trumpet and cornet. He was reportedly given the nickname "King" by trombonist Edward "Kid" Ory, when he established himself as the leading performer among the cornetist in the early days of New Orleans jazz. In 1918 he moved to Chicago, where Armstrong joined him four years later. Oliver's group performed and made their first recordings as "King Oliver's Creole Jazz Band" in 1923, then as "King Oliver's Dixie Syncopators" in the 1926-28 period. The work of Oliver and Armstrong put Chicago on the jazz map of the United States.

Oliver later moved to New York where he made some further recordings. In 1930 he did some touring in the South, but his popularity began to decline. Eventually he was forced to give up playing due to dental problems. Oliver died in 1930 in Savannah, Georgia. In 1976 he was elected by the Down Beat Jazz Critics into their Hall of Fame.

JESSE OWENS

Known universally as "The Ebony Antelope," Jesse Owens made history while competing in the collegiate Big Ten Championships at Ann Arbor Michigan on May 25, 1935, when he had what has been called "the greatest single day in the history of men's athletic achievements." In a little over an hour, he tied the world record for the 100-yard dash and surpassed the world record for five other events, including the broad jump, the 220-yard low hurdles, and the 220-yard dash.

Born James Cleveland Owens in Alabama in 1913, Owens moved to Ohio with his family as a child. J.C. Owens, who eventually was nicknamed "Jesse," competed on his high school track team, gaining national recognition for

clocking 10.3 seconds in the 100-meter dash in 1932. While a member of the Ohio State University track team in 1935, he established a world record of 26 feet 8 inches for the running broad jump. The following year he set a new world record of 10.2 seconds for the 100-meter dash.

As a member of the United States track team at the 1936 Olympics in Berlin, Germany, Jesse Owens earned four gold medals. He won the 100-meter dash in 10.3 seconds, equaling the Olympic record; set a new Olympic and world record of 20.7 seconds in the 200-meter dash; and won the running broad jump with a leap of 26 feet 5 inches. He was also a member of the U.S. 400-meter relay team, which set a new Olympic and world record of 39.8 seconds. Despite Owens's outstanding performance, German leader Adolph Hitler refused to present him with the medals he won because he was black. But Owens's victories brought him fame and contributed to the integration of American sports.

From 1940 to 1942, Owens served as national director of physical education for African Americans with the Office of Civil Defense. President Eisenhower named Owens "Ambassador of Sports" in 1955, and he toured the world for the State Department. In 1976, Owens was awarded a Presidential Medal of Freedom. He died of lung cancer in Phoenix, Arizona in 1980.

Jesse Owens in competition in 1924.

SATCHEL PAIGE

Although racial prejudice kept Satchel Paige from playing major league baseball, he was an outstanding player in the Negro leagues. By the time he was finally allowed into the major leagues, following Jackie Robinson's breakthrough, he was already in his mid-forties.

Leroy Robert Paige claimed to have been born in 1906 in Mobile, Alabama. He acquired his nickname, "Satchel," at the age of seven, when he had a job as a porter at the Mobile railroad depot, carrying an especially large number of satchels at one time.

Paige began his career with the Birmingham Black Barons in 1920. For the next two decades, he compiled a phenomenal record pitching for various teams in the Negro League throughout the U.S. In 1933, he won 31 games and lost four. The following year his team won 104 out of 105 games. In 1942, Paige led the Kansas City Monarchs to victory in the Negro World Series. Four years later he helped them win again by allowing only two runs in 93 innings, pitching a string of 64 straight scoreless innings.

When Paige was brought into the majors in 1948, he was past his prime, yet still led the Cleveland Indians to a World Series victory that year. Four years later, while pitching for the St. Louis Browns, he was named to the American League's All-Star team. After his retirement from major league baseball, Paige continued to play until he was 65, traveling throughout the U.S. with exhibition teams. In 1972, he was elected to the Baseball Hall of Fame. Paige died ten years later at the age of 76.

CHARLIE PARKER

Saxophonist Charlie Parker, who helped to create the jazz style known as bebop, was born in Kansas in 1920, an only child. In high school he was introduced to the alto saxophone, and organized a band called the Deans of Swing.

His schooling suffered as he committed most of his time to the saxophone and learning jazz.

Parker first emerged on the jazz scene in Kansas City in 1939, as a member of the Jay McShann Orchestra. It is said that he earned his nickname, "Yardbird"—later shortened to just "Bird"—from the other members of the orchestra because of his love of chicken. When the band ended a tour in New York in 1942, Parker chose to stay, soon finding himself at the center of a new jazz movement known as "bop." In 1944, Parker teamed up with four other jazz greats: trumpeter Dizzy Gillespie, bassist Ray Brown, pianist Thelonius Monk and drummer Max Roach. Together, along with a few other musicians who joined their group, they created bebop, a fast-paced, free-ranging style that changed the face of jazz forever.

When Gillespie left the group in 1945, Parker formed his own combo. Some of their recordings include "Ko Ko, Billie's Bounce," and "Now's the Time," and many others that have become jazz classics. In December of 1945, Parker went on a West Coast tour and introduced California jazz audiences to bebop. During the height of Parker's career, he began having personal problems, suffered a breakdown and for a time was admitted to a psychiatric hospital. He made a complete recovery and returned to performing, enjoying enormous success in the late 1940s. In 1949, a new jazz club opened in New York called "Birdland" in honor of Parker.

By 1951, Parker was drinking heavily and using heroin. Unable to obtain a permit to perform in nightclubs after being busted for drug use, his career went into decline. Parker suffered from a fatal heart attack and died in New York City in 1955, at the age of 35.

GORDON PARKS

Gordon Parks began as a photographer, and went on to become a cinematographer, film director, and writer. He is the author of fifteen books of fiction, nonfiction and poetry; writer of numerous screenplays and director of six films including *Shaft* (1971). Parks is the composer of the ballet *Martin* as well as other musical works and recipient of over fifty awards and honorary degrees for his achievements in photography and the arts.

Gordon Roger Parks was born in Kansas in 1912, the youngest of fifteen children. He was raised in poverty, yet said in his autobiography, *Voices in the Mirror*, that he was "taught how to live honorably and how to die honorably." When his mother died he was sent to live with an aunt in

Minnesota at the age of 16, but soon was sent away and forced to make it on his own. After many years of moving around, doing various jobs playing piano and waiting tables to make ends meet, Parks began to develop a talent for photography. He moved to Chicago where he received support for his work from the South Side Community Center. Parks photographed society matrons as well as the tenements of South Side Chicago, and in 1941 received a fellowship leading to a job as a photographer in the Farm Securities Administration. From there he became a photographer in the Office of Wartime Information's overseas division during World War II.

After the war, Parks moved to New York, working freelance until he was hired by *Life* magazine as a staff photographer in 1949. He also worked in *Life's* European office and lived in Paris for a year. While traveling throughout the world for *Life*, Parks found time to develop his interest in music, writing two musical scores, which were performed in 1953 and 1955. In 1963, Parks published his novel, *The Learning Tree*. His talents as a photographer, cinematographer, film director, and writer were brought together when he directed the film version of *The Learning Tree* in 1968. "Half Past Autumn: The Art of Gordon Parks," a retrospective exhibition showcasing Park's multifaceted career, began a four-year tour throughout the United States in 1997.

ROSA PARKS

Longtime civil rights advocate Rosa Parks is best known for her 1955 refusal to give up her seat to a white man on a Montgomery, Alabama bus. The landmark incident led to the Montgomery Bus Boycott, and was the precursor to the modern civil rights movement.

Rosa Louise McCauley was born in 1913 in Tuskegee, Alabama. She grew up on her grandparent's farm and at the age of 11 was sent to private school at Montgomery Industrial School for girls. In 1932 she married Raymond Parks, a carpenter who was active in the civil rights movement. Rosa attended Alabama State College and worked for the Montgomery Voter's League as well as the National Association for Colored People (NAACP) Youth Council. In 1943, Parks was elected secretary of the Montgomery branch of the NAACP.

In December of 1955, when Parks refused to give up her seat on a public bus to a white passenger, she was arrested for violating local segregation laws. Local civil rights activists decided to use the incident to organize the Montgomery Bus Boycott. Several churches became

involved and formed the Montgomery Improvement Association, which was headed by Dr, Martin Luther King. It was the beginning of King's leadership in the civil rights movement.

Parks has remained active in the NAACP and Southern Christian Leadership Conference. In 1987, she founded the Rosa and Raymond Parks Institute for Self-Development, offering guidance to young African-Americans. She was awarded the NAACP's Spingarn Medal for her contributions in 1970, and the Martin Luther King Award in 1980, as well as an honorary degree from Shaw College.

In 1999, Parks was awarded the Congressional Medal of Honor for her civil rights work and was deemed "an icon for freedom in America."

Rosa Parks at the March on Washington in 1993.

SIDNEY POITIER

Sidney Poitier was the first African American in film history to earn an Academy Award for best actor in a starring role for his work in the 1963 movie *Lilies of the Field*.

Born in Miami, Florida in 1927, Poitier moved to New York as a teenager and took various dishwashing jobs, until he began to develop an interest in acting. After serving time in the U.S. Army, he joined Harlem's American Negro Theater, working with notable black actors Harry Belafonte, Ossie Davis and Ruby Dee, among others.

Poitier's first Broadway role came in 1946, when he appeared in the all-black production of *Lysistrata*. Two years later he appeared in *Anna Lucasta* with Eartha Kitt, then was offered a role in the movie *No Way Out*. This was the beginning of a film career that lasted through the 1950s and 1960s. It was the films *Edge of the City* (1957) and *The Defiant Ones* (1958) that changed Poitier's career and established him as a star.

In 1967, he starred in the controversial film, *Guess Who's Coming to Dinner*, in which he portrayed a man in love with a white woman, meeting her parents for the first time. Other movie credits include *Raisin in the Sun* (1961), *A Patch of Blue* (1965), *To Sir With Love* (1967), *In the Heat of the Night* (1967) and *The Lost Man*.

In the 1970s, Poitier's career turned to producing and directing. *Stir Crazy* (1980), in which he directed Gene Wilder and Richard Pryor, became the highest grossing film by a black director. Poitier has also appeared in made for television films and television specials. Poitier's autobiography, *This Life*, was published in 1980. He has received numerous awards and honors, including the Kennedy Center award for lifetime achievement in the performing arts in 1995.

ADAM CLAYTON POWELL, Jr.

Adam Clayton Powell, Jr. was the first African-American to be elected to Congress when he became representative from the Harlem district in 1945, a position he served until 1970. In 1963, Lyndon Johnson called Powell "one of the most powerful men in America."

Powell was born in 1908 in Connecticut, the son of a Baptist minister. He grew up in New York City, where he attended City College before moving on to Colgate University. Powell returned to New York City to earn his master's degree from Columbia in 1932. In 1931, while still attending school, Powell began to assist his father who was minister of the Abyssian Baptist Church, a powerful Harlem institution. When his father resigned from the clergy in 1937, Powell assumed his position and quickly developed his pulpit into a platform for social and political change. In 1941 Powell was elected to the City Council, where he continued to fight for racial equality in the city.

Four years later he was elected to Congress, where he served 12 terms. In 1961 he was appointed chairman of the House Committee on Education and Labor, and in 1964 he saw passage of the Civil Rights Act, a version of an effort he had attempted to enact several years earlier called the Powell Amendment. Powell died in 1972 in Miami, just two years after losing his final bid for Congress.

COLIN POWELL

Colin Powell in 1989.

United States military leader Colin Powell was born in New York City in 1937, the son of Jamaican immigrants. Upon graduation from New York's City College in 1958, he received a second lieutenant's position in the U.S. Army, and served two tours of duty in the Vietnam war. Powell became a career army officer, rising through the ranks in various positions, becoming President Reagan's national security advisor in 1987. After being promoted to four star general in 1989, he became the first African-American to hold the nation's highest military post: chairman of the Joint Chiefs of Staff.

Powell played a central role in the planning and execution of the invasion of Panama in 1989, and the Persian Gulf War in 1991. Upon retirement from the U.S. Army in 1993, Powell was awarded the Presidential Medal of Freedom. He has been sought after to run for political office, but has announced publicly that he will not pursue any political candidacy. Powell's autobiography, *My American Journey*, was published in 1995.

LEONTYNE PRICE

Leontyne Price performing in 1953.

Opera singer Leontyne Price was the first black soprano to achieve diva status, when she emerged as a major star in the 1950s. She has performed throughout the world for dignitaries, presidents and audiences of all kinds in concerts, operas and solo appearances. *Time* magazine hailed her as "diva di tutte dive" (diva of all divas) when she performed at the 100th Anniversary Gala of the Boston Symphony Orchestra.

Price was born in Mississippi in 1927. After attending college in Ohio on a full music scholarship, she studied at the Julliard School in New York City. Her first professional appearance came in 1952, when she appeared on Broadway in *Four Saints and Three Acts*. She went on to play Bess in the Broadway production of *Porgy and Bess*, for which she won great critical acclaim. Price made her operatic debut in 1955 in a televised presentation of *Tosca*. During the later 1950s, she sang with the San Francisco Opera Company, the Vienna State Opera, La Scala in Milan, the Paris Opera and Covent Garden, among other European opera companies.

Price returned to New York in 1961, where she made her debut with the Metropolitan Opera Company as Leonora in *Il Travatore*. She continued with the Met until her retirement from opera in 1985. Price has garnered 19 Grammy Awards during her 30-plus year recording career and three Emmy awards for her televised performances. In 1989, she was honored with a lifetime Grammy Award.

RICHARD PRYOR

Richard Pryor in 1977.

Actor, director, screenwriter and stand-up comic Richard Pryor is known for his candid presentation of controversial topics. His unique style has influenced a generation of comic performers.

Pryor was born in Illinois in 1940, and grew up in a poor family. After dropping out of high school at the age of 14, he served in the U.S. Army for two years. Pryor sharpened his instinct for humor into a stand-up comedy act that he began performing in nightclubs in the 1960s. During the late 1960s and 1970s, in response to social changes taking place in America, Pryor began to move away from conventional stand-up comedy and draw upon his experiences as an African-American for use as material in his routines. Using issues such as racism, sex and street life, in an open and confrontational manner, Pryor created comedy routines that were hilarious, insightful and often moving.

In 1967, Pryor made his movie debut, performing small roles in several low-budget films until his first major screen role in *Lady Sings the Blues* in 1972. He went on to become one of the biggest box office attractions of the 1970s, appearing in a string of comic adventures teamed with actor Gene Wilder including *Silver Streak* (1976) and *Stir Crazy* (1980). In 1974, he made his screenwriting debut with Mel Brooks' *Blazing Saddles*. He also released two films of his solo shows, *Richard Pryor Live in Concert* (1979), and *Live on the Sunset Strip* (1982). Pryor's career was interrupted in 1980 after he suffered burns to 50 percent of his body, allegedly caused by a drug-related accident. He made a comeback, but multiple sclerosis forced him to retire from performing in the early 1990s. In 1995 he published his autobiography, *Pryor Convictions: And Other Life Sentences*. Although retired, he remains one of America's best recognized and most beloved comics, and in 1998, accompanied by his daughters Rain and Elizabeth, he was awarded the Kennedy Center's first Mark Twain prize for humor.

OTIS REDDING

Singer Otis Redding's name is synonymous with the term soul, music that arose from the black experience in America and represents a blend of gospel, country and rhythm and blues.

Redding was born in Georgia in 1941 and grew up in housing projects, singing in church as a child. After dropping out of high school in order to work and help support his family, he joined Johnny Jenkins and his band the Pinetoppers. In 1962, after a recording with the band at Stax records, Redding was invited to make his first solo record, "These Arms of Mine." Redding did all of his own writing, composing and arranging. His first album, *Otis Redding Sings Soul*, released in 1965, was recorded in just 24 hours and contains the songs, "Respect" (later recorded by Aretha Franklin), "I've Been Loving You Too Long," and "A Change is Gonna Come." The song considered by many to be Redding's greatest, "Try a Little Tenderness," was recorded in 1967.

Although some of Redding's music was popularized by groups such as the Rolling Stones, he was unable to reach a broad audience or break into the *Billboard* Top 20 charts until after his death. Redding died, tragically, at the peak of his career in a plane crash in 1967. When his song "(Sittin' on) The Dock of the Bay" was released later that year, it became Redding's first song to reach number one on the *Billboard* charts and won two 1968 Grammy Awards. Redding was inducted into the Rock and Roll Hall of fame in 1989 and was the 1999 winner of the Grammy Award for Lifetime Achievement.

ISHMAEL REED

Writer Ishmael Reed is one of today's pre-eminent African-American literary figures, often compared to Ralph Ellison and Amiri Baraka.

Reed was born in 1938 in Tennessee, and grew up in Buffalo, New York. After graduating from the University of Buffalo, he moved to New York City, where he edited the weekly newspaper, *Advance*, and co-founded the *East Village Other*, an underground newspaper that achieved a national reputation. He also organized the American Festival of Negro Art.

In 1967 he moved to California and became a professor at University of California, Berkeley. Reed founded Yardbird publishing company in 1971, with the purpose of advancing the works of a variety of ethnic groups and perspectives that may not have been accepted in mainstream publishing. His first novel, *The Free-Lance Pallbearers*, was published in 1967. Other works include *Yellow Back Radio Broke-Down* (1969), *Mumbo Jumbo* (1972), and *Flight to Canada* (1972). In 1978 he was awarded the Lewis H. Michaux Literary Prize by the Studio Museum in Harlem. His published essay collections focus on a variety of controversial social, political and literary topics. He has taught at Harvard, Yale, and Dartmouth colleges, and has been at Berkeley for more than thirty years.

LITTLE RICHARD

Little Richard on television in 1990.

One of the originators of rock and roll music in the late 1950s, or as he himself would declare, *the* only originator, Little Richard was among the first rock and roll musicians to appeal to a broad audience of both black and white teenagers. The combination of his wild, rebellious performance style and fabulously rhythmic music strongly influenced later rock artists, including the Beatles and the Rolling Stones.

Born in Georgia in 1932, Richard Wayne Penniman was one of 12 children. He left home at the age of 13, singing gospel music at carnivals until a white family who owned a rhythm and blues club where he performed adopted him. Little Richard began recording with RCA records at the age of 19. In 1955 he moved to Specialty records where he recorded "Tutti Frutti," his first hit song, now a rock and roll classic. During the next two years he recorded many of the songs for which he is best known: "Long Tall Sally" (1956), "Rip It Up" (1956), "Jenny, Jenny" (1957), and "Good Golly Miss Molly" (1958). At the same time he appeared in three movies: *Don't Knock the Rock* (1956), *The Girl Can't Help It* (1956), and *Mr. Rock and Roll* (1957).

In 1958, Little Richard stopped singing rock and roll, singing only gospel music after becoming an ordained minister of the Seventh Day Adventist Church. He returned to rock and roll in 1964, and performed sporadically, appearing on television and in movies, as well as occasional live performances. In 1979, Little Richard became an evangelical preacher, but in the 1980s he went back to being a rock and roll celebrity. Little Richard was one of the founding members of the Rock and Roll Hall of Fame in Cleveland, and was awarded the 1993 Grammy for Lifetime Achievement.

FAITH RINGGOLD

Painter, sculptor and performance artist Faith Ringgold is known for her boldly political work using nontraditional materials. Her most renowned works are her distinctive "story quilts," which feature paintings on canvas bordered with quilted materials and scraps of fabric with stories handwritten on them, expressing her experiences as an African-American woman. She has exhibited in major museums throughout the world, and her work is in the permanent collections in New York at the Studio Museum in Harlem, the Metropolitan Museum of Art, the Solomon R. Guggenheim Museum, and the Museum of Modern Art.

Ringgold was born in Harlem in 1934. She attended City College of New York where she received her bachelor's degree in 1955 and masters in fine Arts in 1959. Ringgold currently teaches art at University of California, San Diego. In 1972, Ringgold co-founded the advocacy group Women Students and Artists for Black Liberation. A 25-year retrospective of her work was exhibited at the Museum of African-American Art in 1991.

Ringgold wrote and illustrated the children's book, *Tar Beach*, an adaptation of one of her story quilts. The book, which tells the story of a young black girl in New York City who dreams of flying, was named Caldecott Honor Book in 1992 and won the Coretta Scott King Award for Illustration.

Ringgold's other books include *Harriet's Underground Railroad in the Sky*, *My Dream of Martin Luther King* and *The Invisible Princess*. In addition to numerous honorary doctorates for her work, Ringgold received an award from the National Museum of Women in the Arts in 1996 as well as the Solomon R. Guggenheim fellowship for painting and two National Endowment for the Arts awards.

PAUL ROBESON

Although Paul Robeson is best known for his career as a singer and actor, he was also a talented athlete and strong civil rights activist.

Paul Robeson as "Othello" in 1944.

Robeson was born in 1898 in New Jersey, where he grew up. When he entered Rutgers University, he was one of only a few African-Americans at the school, and went on to become a member of Phi Beta Kappa as well as the first black All-American football player. He received a law degree from Columbia University in 1923. The following year, Robeson appeared in Eugene O'Neill's *All Gods Chillun Got Wings* and *The Emperor Jones* in New York City. At the same time, he made his first voice recital, and quickly became one of the most popular concert artists of the day. He continued working in theater and giving concerts throughout the 1920s and 1930s, also appearing in eleven motion pictures, most notably *Showboat* (1936), immortalizing the song "Ol' Man River." By the end of World War II, Robeson had made more than 300 records.

After losing his passport in the late 1940s for refusing to testify against communism in front of Congress, Robeson was unable to travel or perform publicly. He did continue to give many well-attended private concerts, although his career went into decline. Robeson died in Philadelphia in 1972 after a long illness.

BILL "BOJANGLES" ROBINSON

Bill "Bojangles" Robinson was one of the first people to break existing color barriers in the entertainment world and to become a star of stage and screen.

Luther Robinson was born in Virginia in 1878. He acquired the name Bill by switching names with one of his brothers, and was nicknamed "Bojangles" by a friend, meaning "happy go lucky." Robinson began his career in vaudeville doing duo acts with a variety of partners, as most show managers prohibited blacks from performing solo at the time. Among his many creations was the famous Stair Dance, in which he made a different sound with his feet on each step.

From the 1920s into the 1940s, Robinson appeared in a variety of Broadway shows and was featured in 21 movies. His best known films are the three in which he appeared with child actress Shirley Temple—*The Little Colonel* (1935), *The Littlest Rebel* (1935) and *Rebecca of Sunnybrook Farm* (1938). Unofficially called the "Mayor of Harlem," when Robinson died in New York City in 1949, millions gathered along his funeral route while a band in Times Square played "Give My Regards to Broadway."

JACKIE ROBINSON

Jackie Robinson became an icon of desegregation and forever changed professional sports by becoming the first African-American to play baseball in the major leagues when he signed a contract with the Brooklyn Dodgers in 1947.

Jack Roosevelt Robinson was born in Georgia in 1919. An outstanding athlete from an early age, he excelled in football, baseball, basketball and track in high school and college. After graduating from UCLA and spending time in the army, Robinson began playing baseball professionally with the Kansas City Monarchs, a team in the Negro League. At the time there was intense pressure to integrate the Major

League, and the president of the Brooklyn Dodgers decided to choose a new player to be on his team, rather than an established star. He was also looking for an individual who had the character to endure the enormous pressure, public attention and attacks that were sure to come in a racially prejudiced setting. Robinson was selected.

In 1947, Robinson was named Rookie of the Year. Two years later led the National League in stolen bases and was named Most Valuable player in the league. At the time of his retirement from baseball in 1956, Robinson's career batting average was .311 and he had helped the Dodgers win the pennant six times and the World Series once. After his retirement, Robinson became a prominent spokesperson and fund-raiser for the civil rights movement. In 1962 he was elected to the Baseball Hall of Fame in Cooperstown, New York. Robinson died in 1972 in Stamford, Connecticut.

SUGAR RAY ROBINSON

Sugar Ray Robinson was the only boxer in history to become the middleweight champion of the world five times, beginning with his first middleweight title in 1951.

Born Walker Smith in Georgia in 1921, he began boxing as an amateur using the name and union card of retired boxer Ray Robinson in order to qualify for a bout. When a sportswriter described his fighting style as "sweet as sugar," he became known as Sugar Ray Robinson. After a successful amateur career, Robinson won his first professional championship in 1946 when he earned the welterweight title. In 1950, he moved up to middleweight champion when he beat Jake LaMotta in a 13-round knockout. Later that year he lost the middleweight title, and failed in an attempt to earn it back in 1952. Robinson retired from boxing after this loss, but returned to the ring in 1955, regaining the middleweight title later that year by defeating Carl "Bobo" Olson. He lost and won the title back two more times before retiring from boxing permanently in 1960, with a record of 175 victories in 202 professional fights. Robinson died in Culver City, California in 1989. He was inducted into the International Boxing Hall of Fame in 1990.

DIANA ROSS

Diana Ross was one of the most influential recording artists of the Motown era in the 1960s and early 1970s, as well as the disco period of the late 1970s and early 1980. With her captivating vocal style and glamorous appearance, she and her group, the Supremes, became one of the most successful acts in the history of popular music.

Diana Ross

Ross was born in 1944 to a poor family in Detroit, Michigan. In high school she and two friends, Florence Ballard and Mary Wilson, formed a singing group called the Primettes. The group signed a recording contract with Motown Record Company in 1961, changing their name to the Supremes. Between 1964 and 1967, the Supremes recorded many top hits including, "Come See About Me" (1964), "Baby Love," "Stop in the Name of Love" (1965), "You Can't Hurry Love" (1966), and "You Keep Me Hanging On" (1966). Ten of the group's songs became number-one records on the *Billboard* charts. In 1967 Florence Ballard was replaced and the group changed its name to Diana Ross and the Supremes.

Ross left the Supremes and embarked on a solo career in 1970. Some of her most popular songs include "Ain't No Mountain High Enough" (1970), "Love Hangover" (1976) and "Upside Down" (1980). In addition to singing, Ross has acted in movies, appearing as Billie Holiday in *Lady Sings the Blues* (1972), and starring in *Mahogany* (1975) and *The Wiz* (1978). She has continued recording music through the 1980s and 1990s. The Supremes were inducted into the Rock and Roll Hall of Fame in 1998.

WILMA RUDOLPH

Nicknamed the "black gazelle" by the press, Wilma Rudolph was first woman to win three track and field gold medals at a single Olympics at the Rome Games in 1960.

Wilma Glodean Rudolph was born into a poor family in Tennessee in 1940. At the age of four she contracted double pneumonia, scarlet fever and polio which left her frail and partially handicapped. She was not able to walk normally until the age of 11. Determined to overcome her childhood difficulties, Rudolph became an outstanding athlete in high school. Competing at the 1956 Olympics in Melbourne, Australia at the age of 16 she helped the U.S. women's track team win the bronze medal in the 4 x 100-meter relay. After earning her degree from Tennessee State University, she joined the 1960 Olympic team, winning the 100-meter and 200-meter dashes and the 4 x 100-meter relay. In 1961 she won the James E. Sullivan Memorial Award awarded annually to the nation's top amateur athlete by the American Athletic Union of the United States.

Rudolph retired from competition that year and went on to become a teacher and coach. She died of a brain tumor in 1994.

BILL RUSSELL

The first African-American to play and coach in the National Basketball Association, Bill Russell led the team to 11 titles while coaching the Boston Celtics. Both during and after his playing career he was an outspoken advocate of equal rights for African-American athletes.

Russell was born in Louisiana in 1934 and grew up in Detroit, Michigan and Oakland, California. He attended University of San Francisco on a basketball scholarship and led his college team to the NCAA championship in 1955 and 1956. When he played at the 1956 Olympic Games in Melbourne, Australia, Russell helped the American basketball team win the gold medal.

After joining the Celtics in 1957, Russell's defensive playing capabilities helped them become one of the most successful teams in the history of professional sports, winning the world championship for eight straight years. Russell was named Most Valuable Player five times. During his last three seasons of play, he also coached the team, eventually becoming the first African-American head coach in the NBA. He was inducted into the Basketball Hall of Fame in 1974. His autobiography, *Second Wind: The Memoirs of an Opinionated Man*, was published in 1979.

SONIA SANCHEZ

The early works of poet/playwright Sonia Sanchez reflect the revolutionary social movement of the 1960s. According to critic Mozella G. Mitchell, Sanchez—along with Nikki Giovanni and Don L. Lee—was "one of the leading figures of the new black poetry between 1961 and 1971."

Sanchez was born Wilsonia Driver in Alabama in 1934. Her mother died when she was a year old, and she was taken to New York City where she grew up, attending public schools. After earning her B.A. degree from Hunter College in 1955, Sanchez began a long teaching career. Presently, she is teaching English and Women's Studies at Temple University in Philadelphia.

Sanchez's early poetry collections, published in 1969 and 1970, were inspired by the militant, anti-white stance of Malcolm X. In 1969, she won the P.E.N. Writing Award, and in the following years a National Endowment for the Arts Fellowship and the National Education Association Award. Her 1975 play, *Uh Huh: But How Do It Feel To Us*, explores the tensions between black men and women. Later works are specifically feminist in orientation, reflecting her own personal growth and celebrating women in general. *Homegirls & Handgrenandes*, her 1984 collection of autobiographical prose poems, received an American Book Award from the Before Columbus Foundation.

ARTHUR SCHOMBERG

Historian and bibliographer Arthur Schomberg is best known for founding one of the world's largest collections of African-American culture, the Schomberg Center for Research in Black Culture located in the Harlem branch of the New York Public Library. He also cofounded the Negro Society for Historical Research in New York in 1911, and headed the Negro Academy in Washington, D.C. from 1922 until its dissolution in 1929.

Schomberg was born in 1874 in Puerto Rico, where he attended San Juan's Institute of Instruction to train as a teacher. He studied black literature at St. Thomas College in the Virgin Islands. In 1891, Schomberg came to the United States to teach, and gained prominence through the organizations he headed. During the 1920s, he became a key figure in the Harlem Renaissance, the black cultural movement of new African-American art, literature and music. Over the years he amassed a huge collection of books, manuscripts, and etchings on black Americans, which was purchased by the Carnegie Corporation on 1929 and donated to the New York Public Library. Schomberg became curator of the collection in 1932, a position he held until his death six years later. In 1940, the collection was named in his honor, and later became one of the Research Libraries of the New York Public Library system.

BOBBY SEALE

Bobby Seale founded the Black Panther Party in 1966, in an effort to improve conditions in black communities and protect blacks from police brutality.

Seale was born in Texas in 1936, and grew up in Oakland California. After a brief stint in the U.S. Air Force, he enrolled in Oakland's Merritt College. He and his friend Huey Newton founded the Oakland-based Panthers, writing a ten-point platform for the party, which included ending police brutality, full employment opportunities, improved housing and education, and the exemption of blacks from military service. In addition, the party advocated armed retaliation in response to acts of violence against blacks.

Acting as the national spokesman for the party, Seale organized many community-based activities as well as demonstrations and protests, which resulted in his arrest on several occasions. When the party began to deteriorate in the early 1970s, Seale decided to work within the system and ran for mayor of Oakland, earning 40 percent of the vote in 1973. He left the Black Panthers a year later. In addition to founding another organization called R.E.A.C.H., which combined community activism with environmentalism, Seale has written two books about his political experiences and one cookbook.

BETTY SHABAZZ

Civil rights leader and educator Betty Shabazz first gained prominence as the wife of slain Black Nationalist Malcolm X. Over the years she managed to raise six daughters, and create a legacy of her own.

Born Betty Sanders in 1936, Shabazz grew up in Detroit. After high school she attended Tuskegee University in Alabama, but left to go to nursing school in New York. She met Malcolm X during her junior year, and the two were married in 1958. In 1965, Malcolm was assassinated, leaving Betty a widow at the age of 28. Pregnant with twins at the time, she was left to raise her children on her own, with little money.

Betty Shabazz in 1996.

Determined to complete her education, Shabazz earned her nursing certification, and went on to obtain a B.A. in public health education. In 1975 she received her Ph.D. in education from the University of Massachusetts. Shabazz became a professor of health administration at Medgar Evers College in New York, also serving as the college's director of institutional advancement and public relations. A public figure, Shabazz gave speeches throughout the country advocating education and health care for disadvantaged children, as well as continuing her husband's message of self-determination for African-Americans. She received many honors, awards and tributes for her activism and service to the black community. Shabazz died in June of 1997 from injuries resulting from a fire that was set in her apartment by her grandson.

GEORGE SHIRLEY

Portrait of George Shirley in 1961.

Opera singer George Shirley was the first African-American male to perform leading roles with New York's Metropolitan Opera Company.

Shirley was born in Indianapolis in 1934 and moved to Detroit as a child, where he played the baritone horn in a community band. He graduated from Wayne State University with a bachelor's degree in music education in 1955. After serving in the army, he made his operatic debut in 1959 performing in *Die Fledermaus* with the Turnau players at Woodstock. A year later he made his Italian debut in Puccini's *La Bohème*. In 1961, Shirley's career got a big boost when he won the Metropolitan Opera auditions. He made his debut at Carnegie Hall in 1963, singing in Massenet's *La Navarraise*. Over the years he has been a favorite at the Met, singing with many of the company's leading divas. After recording his own performances and encouraging other opera singers to do the same, he started a radio program about African-Americans in classical music.

O.J. SIMPSON

Orenthal James Simpson, nicknamed "the Juice," was one of professional football's leading ground gainers,

becoming the first running back to gain more than 2,000 yards in one season in 1973.

Born in San Francisco in 1947, Simpson was a star athlete in high school. He earned an athletic scholarship from University of Southern California in 1967, where he set a world record in the 440-yard run as a member of the USC relay team his first year. In 1968, Simpson won college football's Heisman trophy for outstanding player. Upon graduating in 1969, he signed with the Buffalo Bills, and achieved his first rushing title three years later. Simpson's best season came in 1973, when he gained 2,003 yards to break the single season record set by Jim Brown 10 years earlier. That year he received the league's Player of the Year award, which he also earned in 1972 and 1975. After nine seasons with the Bills, he was traded to his hometown San Francisco 49ers, where he played for two seasons before retiring in 1979.

Since retiring from football, Simpson has appeared in several feature films, and has worked as a sports commentator for ABC-TV and NBC-TV. He was inducted into the Football Hall of Fame in 1985. In 1995, a jury found Simpson not guilty of murdering his ex-wife and her male companion after they had been found brutally slain outside her home in 1994.

BESSIE SMITH

The Empress of the Blues in 1936.

Known as the "Empress of the Blues," Bessie Smith was one of the founding mothers of blues music, a sound evolved from African-American spirituals and work songs, and which became the foundation for jazz.

Born in Tennessee in 1894, Smith was orphaned at the age of seven and forced to sing on the streets of Chattanooga for spare change. Her professional career began in 1912, when she joined a traveling show and worked with blues great Ma Rainey. In 1923 she signed a recording contract with Columbia. Her first record, "Down Hearted Blues," sold more than a million copies, and she became the highest paid black performer in the United States. Before long she had some of the best jazz players of the time doing her background, including Louis Armstrong. By 1927 she had become the highest paid black artist in the world. During the 1920s, she was headlining at New York's Lafayette Theater, as well as touring the South with her own revue called the Harlem Frolics. Smith also had a talent for acting and appeared in the 1920 film *St. Louis Blues*.

With the arrival of the Great Depression in the 1930s, musical tastes began to change and Smith's music began to decline in popularity. Smith made her last recording for Columbia in 1931, touring from then on as a "single." In September of 1937, while on tour in Mississippi, Smith was fatally injured in an automobile accident.

WILL SMITH

A multitalented performer, Will Smith is a young triple threat who has achieved fame as a television actor, a Grammy-winning musician, and a big-screen action hero.

Willard Smith was born in 1968 in Philadelphia, where he grew up. He earned the nickname "Prince" from his grade school teachers, who he managed to charm from at a very young age. "Fresh" was added later. Smith began rapping at the age of twelve, teaming up with a friend and performing as DJ Jazzy Jeff and Fresh Prince. The duo produced two platinum albums, including *He's the DJ, I'm the Rapper* (1989) the first rap album to win a Grammy Award.

In 1990, Smith began his television career, starring in a sitcom based on his own life. *The Fresh Prince of "Bel Air,"* produced by Quincy Jones, lasted six seasons. The success of his program gave Smith an entree into Hollywood, and in 1993 he appeared in his first starring role in *Six Degrees of Separation*. He followed up with the smash hit, *Bad Boys*, in 1995, then the blockbuster *Independence Day* a year later. After appearing in the sci-fi hit, *Men in Black*, in 1997, Smith returned to recording. He released his first solo album, *Big Willie Style*, later that year. In 1998 he won the Grammy Award for best Rap Solo Performance for the *Men in Black* soundtrack. At the January 1999 American Music Awards Smith won in three categories: favorite male artist, favorite album, and favorite male soul/R&B artist. His latest film is *Wild, Wild West* (1999).

WILLIAM GRANT STILL

William Grant Still became the first African-American composer to have a symphony performed by an American orchestra, when the Eastman Rochester Philharmonic premiered his *Afro-American Symphony* in 1931.

Born in Mississippi in 1895, Still's mother would not allow him to play ragtime/jazz music because she saw it as irreligious. He entered Wilberforce University as a pre-med student, but became more and more involved in musical pursuits, eventually choosing composing as his profession.

In addition to composing concert music, Still was an arranger and performer of popular music. He was the first African American to conduct a major symphony orchestra, the first African American to have an opera performed by a major opera company, and the first to have an opera performed on national television. *Afro-American Symphony* was, until 1950, the most popular of any symphony composed by an American, having been performed by 38 different orchestras in the United States and Europe in its first twenty years. In his later career, Still directed his work toward young audiences, composing symphonies for children, and writing songs and arrangements for music text books. He died in 1978.

CARL STOKES

In 1965, Carl Stokes became the first African-American elected mayor of a major American City when he won Cleveland's mayoral race. He was also the first African-American to hold high office in all three branches of government—legislative, executive and judicial.

Carl Burton Stokes was born in Cleveland in 1927. His father died when he was two years old, and his widowed mother worked as a domestic to support her two sons. For a time, the family was on welfare. Stokes dropped out of high school and worked at a foundry to contribute to the family income. After serving time in the Army, he returned to high school, earned his diploma and enrolled in college. In 1954 he received his bachelor's degree from University of Minnesota. Two years later he earned his law degree from night law school in Cleveland.

Stokes's political career began in 1962, when he became the first African-American Democrat elected to the Ohio legislature. Three years later he ran for mayor as an Independent, nearly pulling off an upset in a predominantly white electorate. After winning in 1967 on the Democratic ticket, Stokes served two terms and retired from politics in 1971 to pursue a career in journalism.

In 1972, Stokes became the first black news anchor in the New York City area. He worked for WNBC television for eight years before returning to Cleveland in 1981 to pursue a law career, serving as general counsel to the United Auto Workers. In 1983, Stokes was elected a municipal court judge, a position he served until 1994, when President Clinton appointed him ambassador to Seychelles, a cluster of islands in the Indian Ocean.

MARY CHURCH TERRELL

Mary Church Terrell was a key figure in the founding of the National Association of Colored People in 1909 and 1910. She devoted her life to educating people about civil rights, women's rights and black history. She is particularly well known for her contribution to the struggle for the rights of women of African descent.

Terrell was born in 1863 in Tennessee. Her parents had been born into slavery, but worked their way up to become one of the wealthier families in Memphis. Mary Church Terrell became one of the first black women to complete a college education when she graduated from Ohio's Oberlin College in 1884. Four years later she also earned her master's degree from Oberlin. In 1895, Terrell was appointed to the Board of Education in Washington, D.C., a post she held until 1901, then again from 1906 to 1911. She helped organize the Colored Women's League, which later became the National Association for Colored Women, serving as the organization's first president in 1896. Terrell also belonged to the National American Woman Suffrage Association, a group campaigning for a woman's right to vote.

In 1904, she served as part of the American delegation at the International Congress of Women held in Berlin, Germany. After women won the right to vote in 1920, she became active in the Republican Party, often organizing black women for various Republican campaigns. Her autobiography, *A Colored Woman in a White World*, was published in 1940. Until her death in 1954, Mary Church Terrell continued her fight for equal rights for women and African-Americans.

CLARENCE THOMAS

Associate Justice Clarence Thomas was named to the Supreme Court by President Bush in 1991, after a long and controversial hearing.

Thomas was born in 1948 in Georgia, where he grew up. After graduating from Holy Cross College, he earned his J.D. from Yale University. From 1974 to 1977 Thomas was assistant attorney general of the state of Missouri. He was appointed assistant secretary for civil rights in the U.S. Department of Education in 1981, and chairman of the federal Equal Employment Opportunity in 1982. While serving these positions, Thomas became known as an outspoken black conservative, often opposing legislation enacting minority preference programs. Prior to his Supreme Court nomination, he served on the U.S. Court of appeals for the District of Columbia.

Initially, controversy surrounded Thomas's Supreme Court nomination when he was attacked by liberal and civil rights organizations for his conservative views. The nomination became more dramatic when Anita Hill, a law professor and former colleague of Thomas, accused him of sexual harassment. The confirmations drew a nationwide TV audience as Hill brought her charges before the Senate nominating committee and Thomas repeatedly denied them. In the end, the senate confirmed Thomas's appointment to the Supreme Court by a vote of 52–48.

JEAN TOOMER

Writer Jean Toomer earned celebrity as one of the major figures of the Harlem Renaissance with his novel *Cane* (1923), a story focusing on the African American spirit, and often considered a masterpiece.

Nathan Eugene Toomer was born in Washington D.C in 1894. He was raised in the home of his grandparents, a prominent Louisiana political family. During his college years, Toomer attended various universities, with several different majors, but never stayed long in any one in particular. In 1921, he became the principal of an industrial/agricultural school in Georgia. It was while living in the rural South that Toomer wrote *Cane*, which focused on the conflicts of social change in the Black south. His most famous work after *Cane* was the poem "Blue Meridian"(1936), a spiritual message of a new American culture with no racial boundaries.

Years later, Toomer changed direction, following a spiritual journey that led him to be a follower of the Russian mystic Georgi Gurdjieff. At the end of his life, Toomer became a Quaker recluse and died in 1967 in Pennsylvania. A collection of his prose and poetry, *The Wayward and the Seeking*, was published in 1980.

WALTER J. TURNBULL

Dr. Walter J. Turnbull created the Harlem Boys Choir 30 years ago, when he gathered 20 youngsters in the basement of Harlem's Ephesus Church.

The choir went from being an ensemble performing at church services to a major concert attraction. With its repertoire of Bach chorales, Mozart, spirituals and hymns, the choir quickly became the pride of the area.

By the end of 1979, both a touring Harlem Boys Choir and the Girls Choir of Harlem had been established. Turnbull went on to establish the Choir Academy of Harlem, and on-site school serving grades 4 through 8. He and the choir give inner-city children a chance to succeed, most of whom come from low income homes. Turbull's program motivates children through music to become disciplined, confident and successful adults. The choir has achieved international success. Dr. Turnbull received the Heinz Award in the Arts and Humanities in 1998.

TINA TURNER

Entertainer Tina Turner became known to audiences worldwide in the 1960s as lead singer of the group, the Ike and Tina Turner Revue. With a career spanning four decades, she remains one of the hottest performers in the world today.

Turner was born Anna Mae Bullock in Tennessee in 1939. A shy child by nature, she began singing and dancing as a schoolgirl. In 1956, Anna Mae was taken with her sister to live in St. Louis with her mother. At a local nightclub, the girls met bandleader Ike Turner and Anna Mae joined Ike's band, the Kings of Rhythm, using the name "Little Anna." When the couple married in 1958, Anna changed her name to Tina. The group's first single, "A Fool For Love," with Tina as lead singer, was a huge hit, selling 800,000 copies. Under Ike's supervision, they became the Ike and Tina Turner Revue, performing a blend of gospel, rock, blues, and country music. In 1960, the Turners signed a contract with Sue Records, and over the next few years placed five songs on the *Billboard* magazine R&B top ten charts, including "It's Gonna Work Out Fine," "River Deep, Mountain High," and "Proud Mary."

After divorcing Ike in 1976, Tina began a solo career. Her 1983 recording of "Ball of Confusion" led to a contract with Columbia Records with whom she recorded "Let's Stay together," "What's Love Got to Do With It," "Better Be

Good to Me," and the album *Private Dancer*, which included the single hit of the same name. Her second solo album, *Break Every Rule*, was recorded a year later. In 1985, Turner won two Grammy awards for "What's Love Got to Do With It," and another in 1989 for her album *Tina Live in Europe*. In addition, Turner developed an acting career, appearing in the film version of the rock opera *Tommy*, in 1975, and *Mad Max Beyond Thunderdome* in 1985. Tina and Ike Turner were inducted into the Rock and Roll Hall of Fame in 1991.

Tina Turner in concert, 1987.

SARA VAUGHAN

Called "the Divine One" by her fans, jazz singer Sarah Vaughn was born in 1924 in New Jersey. Vaughn first began singing with her church choir, becoming the organ accompanist at the age of twelve. In 1942, she entered, and won, a contest at Harlem's Apollo Theater, which led to the opportunity to join Earl Hines's big band as a pianist and singer. In the band she worked with jazz greats Dizzy Gillespie and Charlie Parker, and later became the only singer to record with Dizzy and "Bird" together. When Billy Eckstein formed his orchestra, the three joined together.

Vaughn began her solo career in 1946, performing and touring with small groups. She recorded many popular tunes in addition to jazz, including numerous songs by Duke Ellington and George Gershwin. Her trademark songs included "Lullaby of Birdland," "Misty," and "Lover Man."

In 1982 she won a Grammy Award for best female jazz vocal performance for her album *Gershwin Live!* Some say that Vaughn's work improved as she got older. She lost none of her amazing voice range, while her command of interpretation grew. Vaughn died in Los Angeles in 1990.

ALICE WALKER

Alice Walker's many novels and books of poetry have earned high acclaim, her most celebrated the 1982 novel *The Color Purple*, which won an American Book Award and a Pulitzer Prize for literature.

Born Alice Malsenior Walker in Georgia in 1944, Walker attended Spelman College in Atlanta and earned her degree from Sarah Lawrence College in New York in 1965. During college she was deeply involved in the civil rights movement. Upon graduating Walker worked for New York City's Welfare Department before beginning a career as a writer and teacher. Her early experiences provided much of the themes for her first work of poetry, *Once*, which is said to have been written during a single week in 1964. Themes of the black experience, racism, black life in American and Africa are present in most of her writing.

Walker's first novel, *The Third Life of Grange Copeland*, was published in 1970. During the early 1970s she published *Five Poems, Revolutionary petunias and Other Poems*, and *In Love and Trouble: Stories of Black Women*, while teaching at Wellesley College and the University of Massachusetts. Next came *Goodnight, Wee Willie, I'll See You in the Morning* (1979), and *You Can't Keep a Good Woman Down* (1981). Other works by Walker include *Meridian* (1976), the essay collection *In Search of Our Mother's Gardens: Womanist Prose* (1983) and *Living by the Word: Selected Writings, 1973–1987* (1988). In 1984, Walker founded Wild Tree Press, which she directed for several years.

When *The Color Purple* was made into a movie in 1985, Walker acted as a consultant. The film version received several Academy Award nominations. Both the book and the movie created controversy over Walker's portrayal of black men. Her 1993 novel, *Possessing the Secret of Joy*, about the practice of female genital mutilation in Africa, also generated controversy among critics. Walker continues to be an activist, writer and teacher, and has won many awards and honors for her work.

MADAME C.J. WALKER

Madame C.J. Walker changed black beauty culture with her hair straightening inventions. Her successful line of beauty products made her the first African-American woman millionaire.

Madame Walker was born Sarah Breedlove McWilliams to indigent farmers in Louisiana in 1867. Her parents died while she was still young, and she went to live with her older sister. At the age of 14, she married and soon gave birth to a daughter. After her husband died when she was only 20, Walker moved to Missouri, where she worked as a laundress. In 1905, she began working on a formula that could be used by black women to straighten their hair. Walker invented a relaxer that could be used with a straightening comb, as well as other beauty products specifically for black women.

In 1906 she moved her business to Denver, where she married Charles Walker and began more aggressive marketing of her products. Walker was the first woman to organize supplies for black hair preparations, develop a steel comb with teeth spaced to comb the strands, place the comb on a hot stove, send the products through the mail, organize door-to-door sales staff, and develop her own beauty school. In 1908, she moved to Pittsburgh with her daughter, Lelia, and set up Lelia College to train cosmetologists in the Walker method. She later moved the company headquarters to Indianapolis, with business operations in New York. Due to Walker's success, many black women have followed her lead and set up their own businesses for black beauty products and hair straighteners. Walker made donations to the NAACP, the colored YMCA, and poor people everywhere. She set up scholarship funds for young women at several colleges and universities, as well as organizing her sales staff to perform community service. Walker died in 1919 at her home in New York.

MAGGIE LENA WALKER

In 1903 Maggie Lena Walker became the first female bank president in the United States when she founded the St. Luke Penny Savings Bank in Richmond, Virginia. A committed philanthropist and civil rights supporter, Walker used the bank's funds to benefit the black community in many ways.

Walker was born in Richmond in 1867 to parents who worked as domestic help for a wealthy white family. Her father died when she was very young and her mother had to support her two children by taking in laundry. By helping her mother from the time she was a small girl, Walker learned the value of hard work and self-reliance. She was an excellent student and began working as a teacher following her graduation from high school in 1883. After marrying in 1886, Walker stopped teaching and devoted herself to the Independent Order of St. Luke (IOSL), a black mutual aid society, for which she became grand secretary in 1890.

In 1902, Walker founded *The St. Luke Herald* newspaper. The following year, Walker convinced the administrators of the IOSL to establish the St. Luke Penny Savings Bank, with the premise that black customers deposit their pennies and nickels, eventually building up enough capital for the bank to finance their home purchases. By 1920 the bank had financed 645 black-owned homes, and by 1924 the IOSL's total assets had risen to $3.5 million. Walker managed the bank so effectively that St. Luke Penny Savings survived the Great Depression and still exists today as Consolidated Bank and Trust Company. Maggie Lena Walker died in Richmond in 1934.

FATS WALLER

A major figure in American music, Thomas Wright Waller was born in New York in 1904, one of 11 children of a Baptist clergyman and he wife. Waller began piano lessons at the age of six, playing mostly by ear rather than following

Fats Waller in 1943.

his lessons. A large child who grew to be six feet tall and weigh over 280 pounds, he was affectionately dubbed "Fats" by his classmates.

During his teens he convinced his father to allow him to drop out of school to pursue his musical career. Waller began playing piano at Harlem's Lincoln Theater in 1919, and soon established himself as one of New York's top pianists. His earliest recordings were "Birmingham Blues"(1922) and "Muscle Shoals Blues" (1922). At the time he also worked in radio, playing piano and singing for WHN in New York City. When Waller began writing songs in 1924, his second composition, "Squeeze Me," became a big hit. Others include "Ain't Misbehavin'," "Honeysuckle Rose," "Blue Turning Gray Over You," and "The Jitterbug Waltz." By the end of the decade he had written a total of 400 songs, including scores for the Broadway shows *Keep Shufflin'* (1928) and *Hot Chocolates* (1929).

Waller's career continued to flourish in the 1930s, and by the middle of the decade he had become an international star. He toured Europe and appeared in several feature-length films with his band Fats Waller's Rhythm, including *King of Burlesque* (1935), *Hooray for Love!* (1935), and *Stormy Weather* (1943). In 1943, at the height of his fame, he died of pneumonia in Kansas City on his way home after an arduous West Coast tour. The 1978 Broadway musical *Ain't Misbehavin'*, a tribute to Waller based on his compositions, won three Tony Awards, including Best Musical.

BOOKER T. WASHINGTON

Educator Booker T. Washington is best known as founder of Alabama's Tuskegee Institute in 1881, a model for black self-improvement through education. The first school of its kind for African-Americans, Tuskegee students were taught a trade, as well as academic subjects. The first students were also required to help build the school, making bricks, putting together the school buildings and raising food for the school. Washington's belief that African Americans should concentrate their efforts on learning a trade so that they could become self-supporting, made him a controversial figure. Many influential black leaders, including W.E.B DuBois and Henry McNeal Turner, among others, disagreed with his views, believing that African-Americans should demand political power and social equality, rather than focusing on self-improvement as a means to success.

Washington was born on a Virginia farm in 1856, the son of a slave cook and an unknown white man. His mother married a slave named Washington Ferguson, and Booker took his name when he enrolled in school after emancipation in 1865. After graduating from agricultural school with honors,

Washington began teaching and continued his education at a school with an all academic curriculum. The two different educational experiences convinced Washington of the need to learn practical skills and a trade in addition to traditional schooling. After building the Tuskegee Institute with the help of the students, the school's influence began to grow and attract nationwide attention. By 1915, Tuskegee had an endowment of nearly two million dollars.

Washington went on to become one of the most powerful men in the South. He was in demand as a speaker throughout the country and became an influential advisor to President Theodore Roosevelt. His fame grew further with the publication of his autobiography, *Up From Slavery*, in 1902. Washington died in 1915 in Tuskegee. After his death he became the first African-American to be commemorated on a postage stamp.

DENZEL WASHINGTON

When Denzel Washington won an Academy Award for his role in the 1989 film *Glory*, he became only the fifth African-American to win an Oscar.

Washington was born in 1954 in Mt. Vernon, New York, where he grew up. He attended a private prep school in upstate New York before entering Fordham University in Manhattan. After graduating from college in 1977, he trained at the American Conservatory Theater in San Francisco. Washington appeared in numerous stage productions before making his film debut in *Carbon Copy* in 1981. He then gained critical acclaim for his small, but crucial, role in *A Soldier's Story* (1984). In his early career, he gained rcognition among a wide audience with his role as a doctor on the television drama *St. Elsewhere* (1982–1988).

His performance in the 1987 film *Cry Freedom* earned him an Academy award nomination and the NAACP's Image Award for Best Supporting Actor. In 1992, he played the leading role in *Malcolm X*, based on the life of the slain African Nationalist leader. Other film credits include *Mo' Better Blues* (1990), *The Pelican Brief* (1993), *Philadelphia* (1993), *The Crimson Tide* (1995), *Devil in a Blue Dress* (1995), *The Preacher's Wife* (1996) and *He Got Game* (1998). Washington is booked for roles through the year 2000, and was listed in a 1998 Harris Poll as the tenth most popular movie star. Despite the demands of his career, he donates large amounts of time and money to humanitarian causes. In 1997 he won an award from the Los Angeles Urban League for outstanding community activities.

DINAH WASHINGTON

Singer Dinah Washington, known as the "Mother of Soul," influenced many later artists, including the "Queen of Soul," Aretha Franklin.

Born Ruth Lee Jones in Alabama in 1924, Washington first began singing gospel in church. Her professional career was launched by a triumphant performance in an amateur contest at Chicago's Regal Theater. In 1943 she joined Lionel Hampton's band as lead singer. When she was discovered by composer and music critic Leonard Feather, the two created several hit songs, including "Salty Papa Blues," "Baby Get Lost," "Evil Gal Blues," and her two best known: "What a Difference a Day Makes" and "Unforgettable." Acclaimed by blues, jazz, gospel and pop audiences alike, Washington died in 1963 from an overdose of sleeping pills. Aretha Franklin dedicated one of her early albums to her, calling it *Unforgettable*.

ETHEL WATERS

Ethel Waters began a 40-year performing career as a nightclub singer in the early 1920s, and went on to become a recording and Broadway star, as well as appearing in films and on television.

Waters was born in 1900 in Pennsylvania, where she grew up in a red-light district, running errands for pimps and prostitutes as a child. She worked briefly as a chambermaid and laundress before she began singing in nightclubs in Baltimore, then established her singing career in New York. Known in the early days as "Sweet Mamma Stringbean," she was a sexy, boisterous singer. In 1925 she signed a 10-year contract with Columbia records. During that period she introduced several hit songs, including "Dinah," "Stormy Weather," and "Am I Blue?" Waters made her Broadway debut in 1927 in the all-black revue *Africana*, and went on to appear in many Broadway productions during the 1930s and 1940s, including *Blackbirds* (1930), *Rhapsody in Black* (1931 & 32), and *Tales of Manhattan* (1942), among others.

In 1939, Waters gave her first dramatic stage performance in the play *Mamba's Daughters*. Her next dramatic role was in the 1950 play, *A Member of the Wedding*. Prior to 1930, her film roles had been mostly risque singing parts, but she did show her more sophisticated style in her later film work, including the 1943 movies *Stage Door Canteen*, and *Cabin in the Sky*. During the 1950s, Waters appeared on television specials and series programs. She spent the last decade of her career singing with the Reverend Billy Graham's religious-revival tours. Waters died in Connecticut in 1977.

MUDDY WATERS

Muddy Waters epitomized the style of music known as "Chicago" Blues. Known for his amplified sound and early use of the electric guitar, Waters was one of the most influential musicians of the twentieth century, inspiring everyone from The Rolling Stones (who took their name from Waters' song "Rolling Stone") and Jimi Hendrix to modern jazz, rock and blues musicians.

Born McKinley Morganfield in 1915 in Rolling Fork, Mississippi, he was sent to live with his grandmother at the age of three following his mother's death. He got the name "Muddy Waters" from his grandmother, who used to scold him for playing in the mud as a child. His first instrument was the harmonica, and he learned to play the guitar soon after. Waters made his first recording for folk historians Alan and John Lomax in 1941 for the Library of Congress. In 1943, he moved to Chicago to become a professional musician. He soon landed a record deal with Aristocrat Records, and in 1947 he released his first hit, "I Can't Be Satisfied." Other hits followed, such as "Rolling Stone," "Louisiana Blues," "Long Distance Call," "Honey Bee," "Baby, Please Don't Go," and "I'm Ready." Muddy Waters died in Chicago in 1984.

FAYE WATTLETON

One of the most influential women in the fight for reproductive rights in America, Faye Wattleton served as president of Planned Parenthood Federation of America (PPFA) from 1978 to 1992. While there, she became a major figure in the national debate over reproductive rights and contributed to the development of family planning policies of governments worldwide.

Wattleton was born in 1943 in St. Louis, Missouri. Her mother was a minister in the Church of God, and did not believe in birth control or abortion. Although the family was poor, they strongly believed in helping those less fortunate. Wattleton entered nursing school at Ohio State University at the age of sixteen, where she earned a bachelor's degree, then did post-graduate work in maternal and infant care. She earned her certification as a nurse-midwife from New York's Columbia University in 1967. In 1970 she became executive director of Planned Parenthood in Dayton, Ohio, also serving as chairwoman of the National Executive Director's Council of PPFA.

During the years of the Reagan presidency, when Wattleton was president of PPFA, individual rights to birth control and abortion became jeopardized by proposed legislation threatening federally funded family planning programs and clinics. Wattleton fought hard to maintain freedom of choice for all women, regardless of economic status, and to keep family planning on the national agenda. Under her leadership, the number of clients at Planned Parenthood tripled and the budget increased from less than $400,000 dollars to over $1 million. In 1989, Wattleton received the American Public Health Association Award of Excellence, the World Society Population Medal and the Congressional Black Caucus Foundation Humanitarian Award. She has received numerous other citations and honorary degrees for her contributions to women's health and has continued her fight for an individual's right to reproductive freedom since her retirement from PPFA in 1992.

ANDRE WATTS

Andre Watts was the first African-American concert pianist to achieve international stardom. He came to national prominence at the age of 16, playing under conductor Leonard Bernstein with the New York Philharmonic Orchestra.

Watts was born in Germany in 1946, to a Hungarian mother and American G.I. father. He spent his first eight years on Army posts in Europe before settling in Philadelphia. By the age of nine he was already performing as a soloist with the Philadelphia Orchestra. After graduating from prep school, he studied at Peabody Conservatory of Music in Baltimore. Watts made his debut in London in 1966, and a month later was the soloist at Lincoln Center's two-day Philharmonic Stravinsky Festival. In the 1970s he performed at the coronation festivities for the Shah of Iran. When he played for Congo's President Mobutu, he was awarded the African Republic's highest honor, the Order of the Zaire Congo. In addition to numerous honorary doctorates, Watts received the Lincoln Center Medallion in 1971 and the National Society of Arts and Letters Gold Medal in 1982. He continues to perform frequently making guest appearances with the Philadelphia Orchestra, Chicago Symphony, Boston Symphony, Cleveland Orchestra, and various European orchestras.

ROBERT WEAVER

Robert Weaver was the first African-American to be appointed a presidential cabinet member when Lyndon Johnson named him the Secretary of Housing and Urban Development in 1969. Prior to his cabinet appointment, he had served in several other high-ranking federal posts, including head of the Housing and Home Finance Agency from 1961 to 1966, and as a member of Franklin D. Roosevelt's "black cabinet."

Weaver was born in 1906 in Washington, D.C., where he grew up and began working as an electrician during his teen years. He went on to earn a Ph.D in economics from Harvard University, where, earlier, his grandfather had been the first African-American to earn a doctorate in dentistry. From 1931 to 1932, Weaver was a professor in economics at the Agricultural and Technical School of North Carolina. He continued concentrating on education during the 1940s and 1950s, lecturing and serving as visiting professor at Northwestern University, Teachers College, Columbia University and at the New York University School of Education. He was also a full professor at the New School for Social Research in New York City. While teaching college, he served as a member of the National Selection Committee for Fulbright Fellowships, as chairman of the Fellowship Committee of the Julius Rosenwald Fund, and as a consultant to the Ford Foundation.

Weaver's political career began in 1955 when he was named New York State's Deputy Rent Commissioner. When he was promoted to State Rent Commissioner at the end of the year, he became the first black to hold a position in the state cabinet in New York. In the early 1960s Weaver served as vice-chairman of the New York City Housing and Redevelopment Board, then headed the Department of Housing and Urban Development until 1968. Weaver resumed his teaching career at New York's Hunter College in 1971, where he stayed until he retired in 1978.

IDA B. WELLS

Best known for her campaign against lynching during the 1890s, Ida B.Wells was head of the Anti-Lynching League as well as a member of the Committee of Forty, which led to the founding of the National Association of Colored People (NAACP).

Wells was born to slaves in Holly Springs, Mississippi in 1862, where she attended Rust University, a high school and industrial school for freed slaves in her hometown. Her parents died while she was a young teenager, and Wells supported herself as a schoolteacher on $25 a month. An activist from early on, Wells was dismissed from her teaching post in Tennessee for her strong criticism of conditions in black schools. In 1885, when she was ordered to move from her first class seat on a railroad car to a car reserved for blacks, she refused and was evicted. She sued for justice and the court ruled in her favor: she was awarded $500 dollars in damages.

When Wells became half owner of the *Memphis Free Speech* newspaper in 1892, she used the paper to begin an anti-lynching campaign by publicly denouncing the lynching of three of her friends. Afterward her offices were destroyed and her life was threatened. Wells chose to move North for her safety and continued her crusade, working with other journalists and editors to publish statistical records of lynchings as well as lecturing extensively in northern cities about the underlying causes of lynching. By the end of her campaign legislation was being adopted in parts of the South to adopt measures against lynch mobs.

In 1898, Wells was elected secretary of the National Afro-American Council, a forerunner to the NAACP, where she served until 1902. She also worked with W. E. B. DuBois in his Niagra Movement, encouraging African-Americans to make more militant civil rights demands. Wells founded the Negro Fellowship League, a community center that helped black men find work, as well as the first women's suffrage organization, the Alpha Suffrage Club of Chicago. Her work on behalf of women's suffrage and civil rights continued until her death in 1931 in Chicago.

CORNELL WEST

Author and philosopher Cornell West gained recognition with the publication of *Race Matters*, his collection of essays dealing with hotly debated issues such as the relationship of blacks to Jews, the 1992 Los Angeles Riots, the failure of black leadership and the nomination of Clarence Thomas to the Supreme Court. Through his writing and teaching, he has helped create a national dialogue on some of the most important issues facing modern society.

West was born in 1953 in Oklahoma, and moved with his family to California while still a child. During his childhood he spent much of his time at the local church and at the offices of the Black Panther Party, where he learned about the concept of Black Power and political revolution. While in high school, West organized a city-wide strike of students in Sacramento, demanding courses in black studies.

West entered Harvard University at the age of 17 and graduated magna cum laude a year early in 1973. He went on to earn a master's degree in philosophy from Princeton University, then served in the faculty at several colleges. In 1977 he began teaching at Union Theological Seminary, where he remained until 1984 when he returned to Princeton as a professor of religion and director of the Afro-American studies department. West returned to Harvard to teach in 1994 and remains a popular scholar and teacher.

DOROTHY WEST

Writer Dorothy West, who was called "the kid" by contemporaries in the Harlem Renaissance such as Langston Hughes, Countee Cullen and Zora Neale Hurston, is the last surviving member of the group.

West was born in Boston in 1907, where she was raised an only child. She began writing stories at the age of seven, and became a regular contributor to *The Boston Post* while growing up. Upon graduating from high school in 1923, she attended Boston University and later the Columbia School of Journalism. During the 1920s West became one of the Harlem Renaissance writers and artists. She published many short stories during that period including. "The Typewriter" (1926), "An Unimportant Man" (1928) and "Prologue to a Life" (1929).

In 1934 and 1937, West founded the literary journals *Challenge* and *New Challenge*. She left New York and moved to her family's home on Martha's Vineyard in 1943, from where she continued to contribute short stories to the *New York Daily News*. Her first novel, *The Living is Easy*, was published in 1948. Although she began a second novel, *The Wedding*, in the 1950s, she was unable to find a publisher at the time. At the urging of Jacqueline Onassis, who met West in 1992 and became her editor, she finished the book and saw it published in 1995. West remains a resident of Martha's Vineyard where she has contributed to the local paper, *The Vineyard Gazette*, since the 1970s.

ROY WILKINS

Portrait of Roy Wilkins, 1958.

Sometimes called "Mr. Civil Rights," Roy Wilkins worked alongside other activists including Dr. Martin Luther King Jr. throughout the civil rights movement of the 1950s and 1960s. He played a major role in the preparation of *Brown v. Board of Education* in 1954 and helped organize the March on Washington in 1963.

Wilkins was born in 1901 in St. Louis, Missouri and grew up in Minnesota. While at the University of Minnesota, where he majored in sociology and minored in journalism, he served as editor of the school paper and edited a black weekly, the St. Paul *Appeal*. Upon graduating, he joined the staff of a leading black weekly, the Kansas City *Call*, where he became managing editor. In 1931 he was appointed assistant executive secretary of the National Association of Colored People (NAACP). From 1934 to 1949, he was editor of *The Crisis*, the official magazine of the NAACP, which previously had been edited by W.E.B DuBois.

During World War II, Wilkins served as consultant to the War Department on black employment. After the war, he continued at the NAACP, where he was appointed executive secretary in 1955. Wilkins served as executive director of the organization from 1965 until his retirement in 1977. For several years Wilkins also served as chairman of the Leadership Conference on Civil Rights. He received numerous awards, including the NAACP's Spingarn Medal for his many years of service, in 1964. Wilkins died in New York in 1981 at the age of 80.

MARY LOU WILLIAMS

Dubbed the "First Lady of Jazz," Mary Lou Williams was one of the first female jazz pianists, composers and arrangers to earn national recognition. A champion of modern jazz, she gave advice to such rising stars as Dizzy Gillespie and Thelonius Monk.

Born Mary Elfrieda Scruggs in 1910 in Georgia. She was raised in Pittsburgh and began performing in public at the age of six. At sixteen she married saxophonist John Williams, with whom she made her record debut. After joining Andy Kirk's band in 1930, which became known as the Twelve Clouds of Joy, she became the band's arranger and pianist. During her time with Kirk's band, she also wrote music for other orchestras. such as Benny Goodman's. In 1942 she formed her own ensemble and became a part of the growing Bebop movement in jazz. Williams earned an international reputation when she lived and toured in Europe between the years 1952 to 1954. In the middle 1950s, she began focusing her career on religious works, including writing a Jazz Mass that was performed in St. Patrick's Cathedral in New York City.

In 1977, Williams became artist-in-residence at North Carolina's Duke University, as well teaching jazz history and performance. She remained at Duke until her death in 1981.

AUGUST WILSON

Award-winning playwright August Wilson was born in Pittsburgh in 1945, one of six children. He dropped out of high school in the ninth grade and educated himself. After briefly serving in the U.S. Army, he co-founded a Pittsburgh-based theater company, Black Horizons on the Hill, in 1968. After moving to St. Paul, Minnesota, in 1978, Wilson established his reputation with a series of award-winning works.

His first play, *Ma Rainey's Black Bottom*, was produced at the Yale Repertory Theater in 1984 before moving to Broadway later that year, where it was named best new play by the New York Drama Critics Circle. His next three major plays, *Fences* (1985), *Joe Turner's Come and Gone* (1986) and *The Piano Lesson* (1987), followed a similar pattern: premiering at the Yale Rep, moving to Broadway and being chosen best new play by the New York Drama Critics Circle. In addition, *Fences* and *The Piano Lesson* both won the Pulitzer Prize for best drama. Other plays include *Jitney*, *Fullerton Street*, *Two Trains Running*, and *Seven Guitars*. Wilson received an honorary degree from Yale University in 1986.

FLIP WILSON

Clerow Wilson was born in Jersey City, New Jersey, in 1933. After quitting school at 16, he joined the Air Force, where he earned the nickname "Flip" for his humor, which would "flip out" the audience. After his discharge from the Air Force in 1954, he began developing a comedy act while working day jobs.

His break came in 1965 when he made his TV debut on *The Tonight Show*, after which he became a regular on shows such as *The Ed Sullivan Show*, *Laugh-In*, and *Love, American Style*. In 1970 he received his own show. *The Flip Wilson Show* was a hit, and Wilson became, along with Bill Cosby, one of the first African-American television superstars. Wilson's characters, such as Freddy Johnson, Reverend Leroy, and especially Geraldine (with Wilson in drag) became household names. In 1971, Wilson won Emmy Awards for writing and performing.

In 1974, Wilson left the show so he could spend more time with his children. Although he starred in the 1984 quiz show *People Are Funny* and the 1985 sitcom *Charlie & Company*, both were short-lived and he largely retired from TV. Flip Wilson died of liver cancer in November, 1998 in his California home.

OPRAH WINFREY

As host and producer of the number one talk show on television, Oprah Winfrey has become one of the most influential figures in the industry. In addition, she has created a legacy that extends beyond television into film, publishing, music, philanthropy, education, health and fitness, as well as social awareness.

Orprah Gail Winfrey was born in Kosciusko, Mississippi in 1954 to unwed teenage parents. Winfrey experienced a difficult childhood that included extreme poverty and sexual abuse. At 14 she gave birth to a stillborn baby. Winfrey's life turned around when she went to live with her father in Nashville, Tennessee. Bright and outgoing, she became a popular and an excellent student at Nashville's East High School, earning a full scholarship to Tennessee State University.

While in college Winfrey became the first and youngest black woman to anchor the news at Nashville's WTVF-TV. After graduating in 1976, she worked as a television newscaster and later as a television talk-show host in Baltimore, Maryland. Seven years later she moved to Chicago to host WLS-TV's local talk show, *People Are Talking*. In less than a year, the show expanded to one hour and was renamed *The Oprah Winfrey Show*. The show, which was known for dealing openly with controversial subjects, was nationally syndicated in 1986. The same year, Oprah formed HARPO Productions to producer her show and other projects. Since entering syndication, *The Oprah Winfrey Show* has remained the number one talk show for twelve consecutive seasons, winning 32 Emmy Awards.

Always interested in acting, Winfrey made her movie debut in 1985 as Sophia in Steven Spielberg's *The Color Purple*, for which she won an Academy Award and a Golden Globe nomination. Her second major film role came in 1998 as Sethe in *Beloved*, based on the novel by Toni Morrison. During the 1990s Winfrey performed in the made-for-television movies *There Are No Children Here* and *The Women of Brewster Place*. Through HARPO Films, Winfrey has a contract with ABC Television Network to produce at least six telefilms, two each year. Her first two projects, *Before Women Had Wings*

Oprah Winfrey at the Daytime Emmy Awards in 1997.

and *The Wedding*, were among the highest rated television movie broadcasts of the 1998-99 season.

In September of 1996, Winfrey began Oprah's Book Club, an on-air reading club designed to encourage her viewers to get excited about reading again. Each of the books selected for the book club to date has become an instant bestseller. Ranked the highest-paid entertainer by *Forbes* magazine in 1997, Winfrey has always contributed to her alma mater,

Tennessee State University, and the Family for Better Lives Foundation, which she created. She has been honored with the George Foster Peabody Individual Achievement Award (1996) and the National Academy of Television Arts and Sciences Lifetime Achievement Award (1998). In June of 1998, Oprah Winfrey was named one of the one hundred most influential people of the twentieth century by *Time* magazine.

STEVIE WONDER

Stevie Wonder, whose voice is recognized throughout the world, has had more top ten pop records than anyone other than the Beatles and Elvis Presley.

The name on Wonder's birth certificate is Steveland Morris, although his father's name is Judkins, which he has also used. Born prematurely in Michigan in 1950, Wonder lost his sight due to complications from an excess of oxygen in his incubator. By the age of two, his musical ability became apparent and at seven he began piano lessons. At the age of ten, Wonder moved with his family to Detroit where he was introduced to record producer Berry Gordy, Jr. His professional career began when Gordy signed him to a five-year contract with his company, which later became Motown Records, and gave him the name of Little Stevie Wonder. Wonder's third single, "Fingertips," became the first in a succession of huge hits when it sold more than a million copies and went straight to number one on the pop charts, remaining there for fifteen weeks. In 1963, he recorded his first album, *Little Stevie Wonder The Twelve-Year-Old Genius*. A number of hit singles followed including: "Uptight (Everything's All Right)" (1965), "I Was Made to Lover Her" (1967), "My Cherie Amour" (1968), and "Yester-Me, Yester-You, Yesterday" (1969). In 1970 he produced his own album, *Signed, Sealed and Delivered*.

After breaking with Motown, Wonder began develop a unique style using electronic instrumentation. In 1972 he released the pioneering album *Music of My Mind*, using Arp and Moog synthesizers and a clavinet. During the 1970s, Wonder earned a total of 14 Grammy Awards for his albums *Talking Book* (1972), *Innervisions* (1973), *Fullfillingess' First Finale* (1974), and *Songs in the Key of Life* (1976). His 1980 album, *Hotter Than July*, featured four hit singles. Two years later Wonder recorded "Ebony and Ivory" with Paul McCartney, and wrote "I Just Called to Say I Love You," the theme song to the movie *The Woman in Red*. Wonder's popularity has remained strong as he continues to release new music and draw large crowds during his frequent tours. He was inducted into the Rock and Roll Hall of Fame in 1989.

GRANVILLE WOODS

Granville Woods is best known as the inventor of more than 60 patented devices including railroad communication systems, electrical railways, automatic air brakes for trains and a third rail system for trains, which is still used today in New York City's subway system.

Woods was born in 1856 in Ohio, and moved to Missouri at the age of 16 to work as a railway fireman and engineer. Although his early education ended when he was ten years old, he later took college-level engineering courses. In his mid-twenties he moved to Cincinnati, where he started Woods Electric Company, a manufacturer of telephones, telegraphs and electrical equipment. In 1884, Woods received his first patent, for a modified boiler furnace that saved on fuel. His second came later that year for a transmitter that sent messages by electricity, a great improvement over the telephones in use then. He sold some of his inventions to American Bell Telephone Company, Westinghouse Air Brake, and General Electric. Between 1884 and 1907, he patented some 35 inventions, some of which improved telephone systems used by trains to communicate with each other and greatly improved railway safety.

In 1890, Woods moved to New York City, where he spent time on his inventions. Because of a court case in which he was sued for accusing a company of stealing his inventions, Wood ran into financial troubles in his later years. Although he eventually won the case, the enormous legal fees involved left him destitute when he died in New York in 1910.

TIGER WOODS

Tiger Woods became the first African-American to win a major golf tournament when he won the Masters Championship in 1997. Woods, whose father is African-American and whose mother is Thai, was also the first Asian-American and the youngest player ever to win the Masters Championship.

Eldrick Woods was born in California in 1975 and nicknamed "Tiger" by his father after a buddy he had served in the Vietnam War with. Woods began playing golf as soon as he could walk, and by the age of three was good enough to shoot a 48 for nine holes. Soon he was touted as a golf prodigy and featured on several television shows. Coached by his father, he was taught form, stance, swing, and—most important—concentration. At 15 he became the youngest player ever to win the United States Golf Association (USGA) Junior National Championship.

In 1992 Woods entered Stanford University, and the same year won his third consecutive USGA Junior National Championship, becoming one of the top players in the amateur circuit. At Stanford he was named Pacific-10 Conference golf player of the year in 1995. Between 1994 and 1996, Woods captured three consecutive U.S. Amateur Championships, after which he turned professional. In his first year as a pro, Woods won two tournaments on the Professional Golfers Association (PGA) tour. When he won the Masters in 1997, he broke several tournament records including the lowest score for 72 holes. That year he won three more PGA tournaments, ending the year as the first player in history to win more than $2 million in prize money. He earned the PGA Player of the Year Award and was named Male Athlete of the Year for 1997 by the Associated Press.

CARTER WOODSON

Known as the Father of Black History, Carter Woodson devoted his life to making "the world see the Negro as a participant rather than a lay figure in history." He is credited as the creator of Black History Month.

Carter Godwin Goodson was born in 1875 to former slaves in rural Virginia. Unable to attend school while he was growing up, due to the need to contribute to the family income, Woodson's education was limited to what he could learn on his own. Despite this, he entered high school at the age of 17 and was able to finish in a year and a half. He then entered Berea College in Kentucky, graduating in 1903. After teaching elementary school for two years, Woodson studied at University if Chicago, where he earned a B.A. and an M.A.. In 1912, he earned his Ph.D from Harvard.

While working in Washington, D.C. schools, in 1915 Woodson founded the Association for the Study of Negro Life and History, which he also directed until his death. The Association's focus was on historical reasearch and to advance the teaching of history. At the same time Woodson founded the *Journal of Negro History*, a quarterly magazine that he edited until his death. In 1926, he organized the first annual Negro History Week, which he promoted heavily through schools, press releases and speaking engagements. This eventually became Black History Month. Among his many books are *Education of the Negro Prior to 1861* (1915), *History of the Negro Church* (1921) and *The Rural Negro* (1930). Woodson died in Washington D.C. of a heart attack in 1950.

RICHARD WRIGHT

Richard Wright's novels and short stories about race relations in the mid-20th century made him perhaps the most eloquent spokesperson for his generation of African-Americans. His best known works are the novel *Native Son* (1940), and his autobiographical memoir, *Black Boy* (1945).

Richard Nathaniel Wright was born in Mississippi in 1908. Raised mostly by relatives, he quit school at the age of 15 and moved to Memphis where he worked at odd jobs and began educating himself. During the Great Depression of the 1930s, Wright worked for the Federal Writer's Project in Chicago. His first book, *Uncle Tom's Children* (1938), won first prize in a competition sponsored by the Project. In 1937, Wright moved to New York where he worked on a Writer's Project guidebook to the city entitled *New York Panorama*. At the same time he published reviews and political essays in Communist party publications. Wright was an active member of the party from the time he was in Chicago, until the 1940s, when he changed his views.

Richard Wright in June, 1939.

When *Native Son* was published in 1939, the book became an immediate sensation among black and white readers alike, helping Wright to become the first black American writer to have a best seller. After moving to France in the 1940s, Wright published several more novels including *The Outsider* (1953) and *The Long Dream* (1958). Two of Wright's works, the short-story collection *Eight Men*, and the novel *Lawd Today*, were published after his death. Wright's non-fiction works include *Black Power* (1954), *The Color Curtain* (1956), *Pagan Spain* (1957), and *American Hunger* (1977), another autobiographical work. In 1941, Wright collaborated with photographer Edwin Rosskam on *12 Million Black Voices*, a folk history of blacks in America. He died of a heart attack in 1960 in Paris, France at the age of 52.

MALCOLM X

Malcolm X in U.S. Capitol Building during discussion of Civil Rights Bill, June 1964.

The most prominent spokesperson of the Nation of Islam during the 1960s, Malcolm X's thinking and writings continue to influence African-American politics today.

Born Malcolm Little in Nebraska in 1925, Malcolm's father, a Baptist minister, was an outspoken follower of black nationalist leader Marcus Garvey. In 1931, when Malcolm was only six years old, his father was murdered after receiving threats from the Ku Klux Klan. His mother was unable to raise her eight children alone, and Malcolm was sent to foster homes, then reform school. After finishing eighth grade, he went to live with his sister in Boston, then moved to New York three years later, where he settled in Harlem.

While living in Harlem, Malcolm developed a drug addiction and a crime-focused lifestyle. In 1946, he was sentenced to 10 years in prison for burglary. It was during his time in prison that Malcolm became interested in the teachings of Elijah Muhammed, the leader of the Black Muslims, also called the Nation of Islam. When he was released from prison in 1952, Malcolm joined a Black Muslim temple and took the name Malcolm X. A dynamic speaker, Malcolm quickly rose in the ranks of the Black Muslims, and in 1954 he was transferred to Harlem to head its mosque.

As his power and influence grew, Malcolm became a threat to Elijah Muhammed, and grew more independent. Malcolm broke with the Nation of Islam in 1964 after being silenced for an irreverent remark he made regarding the assassination of President John F. Kennedy. He started his own group, the Organization of Afro-American Unity (OAAU), a secular black nationalist separatist movement. After a pilgrimage to the Muslim holy city of Mecca, Malcolm renounced his previous teachings that all white people were evil, and began advocating racial solidarity. He adopted the Arabic name El-Hajj Malik El-Shabazz.

On February 21, 1965, while addressing an OOAU rally in New York City, Malcolm was assassinated by men allegedly connected with the Black Muslims.

ANDREW YOUNG

A disciple and close associate of civil rights leader Martin Luther King, Jr., Andrew Young helped to draft the Civil Rights Act of 1964 and the Voting Rights Act of 1965. From 1972 to 1977, he served as the first black congressman from the South since the days of post-Civil War Reconstruction, and was appointed United States Ambassador to the United Nations by President Jimmy Carter in 1977. In 1992, Young was elected mayor of Atlanta, a position he served for eight years.

Andrew Young was born in New Orleans, Louisiana in 1932. Despite being from a well-to-do family, Young was bussed to an all-black school as a child. He graduated from Gilbert Academy, a private high school in New Orleans, when he was only 15. After becoming interested in the ministry, Young earned his divinity degree from the Hartford

Andrew Young in Washington in 1968.

Theological Seminary in Connecticut in 1955 and was ordained a minister of the United Church of Christ.

In 1961, Young moved back to his native South and began working with Dr. Martin Luther King, Jr. He was appointed executive director of King's Southern Christian Leadership Conference in 1964. After King's assassination in 1968, Young decided to enter politics, and was elected U.S. Representative from Georgia in 1972. As U.S ambassador to the United Nations, Young promoted understanding between the U.S. and the nations of black Africa. He resigned in 1979 after a controversy caused by his contacts with the Palestine Liberation Organization. During his term as mayor of Atlanta, Young was regarded as successful by both black and white residents of the city.

WHITNEY YOUNG

Civil Rights leader Whitney Young is best remembered as director of the National Urban League, a position he served from 1961 to 1971, the most turbulent time in civil rights history.

Whitney M. Young, Jr. was born in 1921 at the Lincoln Institute, a private high school for blacks in Kentucky. His father was the first black principal of the school, and his mother was the first black postmaster in Kentucky, and only the second in the United States. Young spent most of his childhood living at the school, and earned a B.S. from Kentucky State College, a historically black institution, in 1941. He then did graduate work at Massachusetts Institute of Technology and received an M.A. in social work from University of Minnesota in 1947.

After serving as the dean of the school of social work at Atlanta University from 1954 to 1961, Young spent one year as a visiting scholar at Harvard University. He became a prominent lecturer and served as president of the National Association of Social Workers as well as the National Conference on Social Welfare. During the Kennedy and Johnson administrations, Young became a part of seven presidential commissions. In 1969, President Johnson awarded him the country's highest civilian award, the Medal of Freedom.

Under Young's leadership, the Urban League became a major force in the struggle for civil rights. In an effort to afford greater opportunities for blacks, Young established relationships with prominent white leaders in business and politics. He was outspoken in his criticism and allied the Urban League with some of its more militant counterparts in an effort to make African-Americans part of the decision-making process. Young published two books, *To Be Equal* (1964), and *Beyond Racism: Building an Open Society* (1969). He died of a heart attack in Lagos, Nigeria in 1971.

A CENTURY OF GREAT AFRICAN-AMERICANS

While the A-to-Z listings include major African-American personalities of the twentieth century, there are dozens of others who deserve a place in this book. Many of them have achieved "firsts" for blacks in America, such as Benjamin O. Davis, the first General in the U.S. Army, Bessie Coleman, the first female African-American to fly an airplane, and Alice Coachman, the first African-American woman to win the Olympic gold medal in track and field. Others have made contributions to the modernization of America in the twentieth century, such as inventor Garret A. Morgan who invented the electric traffic light in 1923 and neuosurgeon Ben Carson, M.D. who in 1987 successfully separated cojoined twins. Others warrant mention for their endeavors in business and the arts, such as William H. Gray III, president of the United Negro College Fund, painter Aaron Douglass, actor Danny Glover, and internationally acclaimed pianist Natalie Hinderas. A brief, and admittedly, incomplete listing follows.

ROBERT ABBOTT

Publishing pioneer Robert Abbott founded the *Chicago Defender* in 1905, and turned it into the country's third largest and most influential black newspaper.

BENNY ANDREWS

Artist Benny Andrews is most noted for directing the Visual Arts Program for the National Endowment for the Arts from 1982 to 1984. Since 1985 he has directed the National Arts program in which children and adults in cities throughout the country exhibit their works and compete for prizes.

TONI BAMBARA

Author and educator Toni Bambara has won numerous awards for her writing and film work, including the 1981 American Book Award for her novel *The Salt Eaters*.

RICHMOND BARTHE

Award-winning sculptor Richard Barthe was the first black person to receive a commission to produce a bust for New York University's Hall of Fame.

BOB BEAMON

Track and field star Bob Beamon won the Olympic gold medal in the long jump in 1968, setting a world record of 29 feet 2 inches, nearly two feet longer than the previous world record.

ROMARE BEARDEN

Called the "Dean of Black Painters," Romare Bearden's unconventional use of artistic materials and unique interpretation of mixed media collage created an intimate view of the African-American experience.

SIDNEY BECHET

Solo saxophonist and clarinetist Sidney Bechet was the first jazz player to achieve recognition on the soprano saxophone, as well as being one of the first to win acceptance in classical circles as a serious musician.

GWENDOLYN BENNETT

As a young writer, Gwendolyn Bennett rose to prominence during the Harlem Renaissance Movement in the early 1920s. She was a contributor to the NAACP's *Crisis* magazine, a columnist for the National Urban League's *Opportunity* magazine, contributing editor of *Fire*—the magazine produced by the writers of the Harlem Renaissance—and head of the Harlem Community Arts Center.

GUION STEWART BLUFORD, Jr.

Guion Bluford became the first African-American astronaut in space when he flew as a mission specialist aboard the space Shuttle Challenger in August, 1983 and October, 1985.

JANE BOLIN

Jane Bolin was educated at Wellesley College, and became the first black woman to receive a law degree from Yale University. Bolin ran unsuccessfully for a Republican seat in the New York State Assembly in 1936, however, she was appointed to the Corporation Counsel's office in New York City soon after. In 1939 New York mayor Fiorello La Guardia appointed Jane Bolin head of the Court of Domestic Relations, making her the first African-American judge in the United States.

JAMES BOOKER

New Orleans piano player James Booker had a career spanning nearly four decades. His long and brilliant recording career included many solo works as well as cooperative works with Fats Domino, Earl King, The Coasters, Ray Charles, Lionel Hampton and Lloyd Price, among others.

WILLIAM STANLEY BRAITHWAITE

Poet and editor William Stanley Braithwaite is credited for acquainting the general reading public with outstanding contemporary poetry through his newspaper column in the *Boston Evening Transcript*, and magazine articles during the first two decades of the twentieth century.

CHARLES BROWN

Blues pianist Charles Brown and his group, the Three Blazers, were stars in the 1940s and 1950s, as part of the new black music that was coming out of post war Los Angeles. The group became one of the premiere examples of a new, more sophisticated rhythm and blues that was replacing jazz as popular music among African-Americans. The group mixed swing, blues and harmony, placing Brown's voice out in front. In 1945 they recorded "Drifting Blues," which became a hit and a template for the new style of music.

JESSE BROWN

Jesse Brown became the first African-American to head the Veteran's Affairs Department as a member of President Clinton's cabinet.

JESSE LEROY BROWN

Jesse Leroy Brown became the first African-American pilot in the United States Naval Reserve in 1949. In 1950 he was the first African-American naval pilot killed in action, at Changjin Reservoir in Korea.

OSCAR BROWN

Songwriter Oscar Brown wrote compositions and lyrics for jazz musicians Max Roach, Nat Adderly and Miles Davis, among others. In 1962 he hosted the television program *Jazz Scene*.

RUTH BROWN

Ruth Brown, who grew up on the Virginia Coast began singing in church and performing as a teenager. Discovered by a club owner in Virginia, she obtained her first booking in Detroit. After a rough start in various clubs, she met the sister of Cab Calloway, who signed her up immediately and helped her career. Brown was signed by Atlantic Records and was among the pioneers who first made R & B music popular. Her first big hit, "So Long," established her as a major talent and led the way to the development of soul music.

STERLING BROWN

Poet, teacher and linguistic historian Sterling Allen Brown earned fame for incorporating dialect, the rhythms of work songs, and the themes of black folk epics into his poems.

WILLIE BROWN

In 1995, Willie L. Brown, Jr. defeated incumbent mayor Frank Jordan to become San Francisco's first African-American mayor. Flamboyant and popular, Brown was reelected to a second term in 1998 and continues to serve today.

JOYCE BRYANT

Soprano Joyce Bryant sang with the New York City Opera for three years, and is best known for her performance in the company's 1961 production of *Porgy and Bess*.

JOHN W. BUBBLES

Considered to be the father of rhythm tap dancing, John Bubbles earned recognition as a partner in the successful 1920s vaudeville team, Buck and Bubbles. During his sixty years in the entertainment industry, Bubbles helped break down racial barriers.

HAYWOOD BURNS

Attorney Haywood Burns was best known for his civil rights work with the Dr. Martin Luther King, Jr., and his defense of Attica prison rioters and black radical Angela Davis. In 1968 he acted as general counsel to Martin Luther King, Jr.'s Poor People's Campaign, while serving under the NAACP Legal Defense and Education Fund. Burns helped found the National Conference of Black Lawyers in 1969, and was its first director. He gained national attention when he won an acquittal for Professor Angela Davis, who was charged with murder and kidnapping in the 1970 San Rafael, California courthouse invasion aimed at freeing black prisoners. In 1998 the New York State Bar Association created the first annual Haywood Burns Memorial Award in honor of his commitment to the struggle for justice.

DIAHANN CARROLL

Actress Diahann Carroll's career was launched in early 1950s when she appeared on a television talent show while in college. She has appeared in many films and stage shows, winning a Tony award in 1962 for *No Strings*, in which she portrayed a high-fashion model. Carroll has also been featured in television series such as *Dynasty*, *Julia*, and *Different World*.

BEN CARSON, M.D.

Detroit neurosurgeon Ben Carson is prominent for his expertise in performing complex neurosurgical procedures, particularly on children. He earned international acclaim for his famous operation in 1987 in which he successfully separated a pair of West German conjoined twins.

ALICE CHILDRESS

Alice Childress's 1952 play, *Gold Through the Trees*, was the first professionally produced play by an African-American woman. She has won numerous awards for her plays and children's books, including an Obie Award for best off-Broadway play in 1956 for *Trouble in Mind*.

ALICE COACHMAN

Alice Coachman became the first African-American woman to capture an Olympic gold medal with her performance in the high jump at the 1948 Games in London, England.

BESSIE COLEMAN

Bessie Coleman was the first African-American woman ever to fly an airplane, the first African-American to earn an international pilot's license, and the first black female stunt pilot.

RALPH COOPER

For many years Ralph Cooper served as MC at Harlem's famed Apollo Theater. Cooper was best known as host of *Amateur Night at the Apollo*, which he conceived and promoted. *Amateur Night* began in 1935 and occurred every Wednesday night, providing a showcase for new and undiscovered performers who could prove their abilities to the Apollo's discriminating audience. The audience consisted of both black and white fans, coming from destinations throughout the world. Ella Fitzgerald, Roberta Flack, Stevie Wonder, Diana Ross and the Jackson Five are all said to have first achieved recognition at the Apollo.

DOROTHY DANDRIDGE

Actress Dorothy Dandridge began performing as a child in the 1930s as one of the Dandridge Sisters, a popular act at Harlem's Cotton Club, and in the movie *Day at the Races* (1937). During the 1940s Dandridge began to perform on her own, beginning a successful night club career that lasted into the 1950s. Her best work, however, was as a film actress. Dandridge became the first African-American actress to receive an Academy Award nomination in 1954 for her role as Carmen in the all-black musical *Carmen Jones*. In 1957 she made a breakthrough in desegregation on screen when she was paired romantically with a white man in the film *Island in the Sun*. In all, Dandridge appeared in over 25 movies. She died from an overdose of a prescription antidepressant in 1965.

ANTHONY DAVIS

Pianist and composer Anthony Davis is active in a variety of media, including operatic, symphonic, choral, chamber, dance, theater and improvised music. His music embodies an intercultural approach drawing upon traditional and current African-American sources as well as Javanese, American minimalism, and European avant-garde. Davis has performed and recorded with a wide variety of musical improvisors. In 1996, he received an Academy Award from the American Academy of Arts and Letters for his work.

BENJAMIN O. DAVIS, Jr.

Benjamin O. Davis, Jr. became the first African-American Air Force general on October 1954, only the second African-American general in the U. S. Armed Forces, after his father, Benjamin O. Davis, Sr.

BENJAMIN O. DAVIS, Sr.

Benjamin O. Davis was the first African-American to reach the rank of general in the U.S. Army when President Franklin D. Roosevelt promoted him to brigadier general in October 1940.

ERIC JEROME DICKEY

Eric Jerome Dickey was born in Memphis, Tennessee, and attended the University of Memphis. He is the best-selling author of the novels *Cheaters*, *Milk in My Coffee*, *Sister Sister* and *Friends and Lovers*, exploring the lives of young African-Americans today. He has also written a screenplay for the movie *Cappuccino*, directed by Craig Ross, Jr.

DAVID DINKINS

After serving as city clerk from 1975 to 1985, David N. Dinkins became New York City's first African-American mayor in November 1989. He served one term.

LARRY DOBY

Larry Doby, with 253 career home-runs, was the first black player in the American Leaue. Born in in 1924 in Camden, South Carolina, he grew up in New Jersey where in high school he starred in baseball, football, basketball and track. Doby was signed up by the Newark Eagles of the Negro League, where he remained until 1947 when he was signed by the Cleveland Indians. His stunning career coincided with that of Jackie Robinson, who preceded him into the major leagues and received most of the publicity. After his retirement, Doby worked for the State Department in Japan as a player, teacher and good-will ambassador, then gave clinics throughout the U.S. on behalf of the Vice President' Council on Physical Fitness, and finally returned to baseball as a coach, minor league instructor, and coach. Doby was elected to the Baseball Hall of Fame by the Veterans Committee in 1998.

AARON DOUGLASS

As a painter, illustrator and muralist, Aaron Douglass achieved recognition in the 1920s and 1930s exhibiting throughout the United States. His murals entitled *Aspects of Negro Life* are displayed at the Schomberg Center in Harlem.

CHARLES RICHARD DREW

Surgeon Charles Richard Drew, born in Washington, D.C. in 1904, was a pioneer in the field of blood transfusion. Drew graduated from Amherst College and received his medical degree from McGill University in Canada. During World War II he created a program for gathering and processing blood supplies that became the model for national blood-bank programs. He continued his work with blood banks until his death in 1950 in an automobile accident.

MARIAN WRIGHT EDELMAN

A graduate of Spelman College and Yale Law School, Marian Edelman became the first African-American woman admitted to the Mississippi state bar. She served as head of the NAACP Legal Defense and Education Fund's office in Mississippi and then as counsel to the Poor People's Campaign in Washington, D.C. She later established the Washington Research Project, concentrating on lobbying for expanded child and family nutrition programs and an expanded Head Start program. In 1973 Edelman founded the Children's Defense Fund, created to bring the plight of poor children to the attention of policy makers and the public. In 1995, Marian Edelman received the Heinz Award in the Human Condition for her work in creating and funding programs to improve children's lives.

ROY ELDRIDGE

Jazz trumpeter Roy Eldridge, known in the world of music as "Little Jazz," played from the late 1920s into the 1970s, in the bands of Fletcher "Smack" Henderson, William "Count" Basie and others. When he joined Gene Krupa's band in 1941, he became the first African-American musician to be featured in a white band as a full member of the band

MIKE ESPY

In 1986, Mike Espy became the first African-American to be elected to the U.S. Congress from Mississippi since the Reconstruction era. In 1993 he was confirmed as Secretary of Agriculture under President Bill Clinton.

JAMES REESE EUROPE

As the most popular bandleader at the turn of the twentieth century, James Reese Europe was dubbed the "King of Jazz." He formed the Clef Club Orchestra at Carnegie Hall in 1910, and had a major influence on the development of jazz in Europe when he directed the 369th Infantry Regimental Band during World War I.

CRYSTAL BIRD FAUSET

Crystal Bird Fauset became the first African-American woman elected to a state legislature in the United States when she was named to the Pennsylvania House of Representatives in November 1938.

GAIL FISHER

Gail Fisher was the first African-American woman to win an Emmy Award, which she was awarded in 1969 for her performance in the television series *Mannix*.

ROBERTA FLACK

Roberta Flack's rendition of "The First Time Ever I Saw Your Face" earned an Emmy Award for Record of the Year in 1971. Her other number-one hits included "Killing Me Softly" (1973) and "Feel Like Makin' Love" (1974).

FLOYD FLAKE

U. S. Representative from New York Floyd Harold Flake was first elected to Congress in 1986. He has served as a member of the House Committee on Banking, Finance and Urban Affairs, the House Committee on Small Business, and the House Committee on Hunger. He was reelected to two additional full terms in 1989 and 1991.

HENRY O. FLIPPER

Born to slave parents in 1856, Henry O. Flipper became the first African-American to graduate from the U.S. Military Academy at West Point in 1877. Following his discharge from the Army in 1882, Flipper became a special agent of the Department of Justice, and in 1922, was appointed Assistant to the Secretary of the Interior. Flipper died in 1940.

T. THOMAS FORTUNE

In 1890, Timothy Thomas Fortune helped organize the National Afro-American League, an organization that foreshadowed the civil rights organizations of the 20th century. A respected journalist, he worked as an editorial writer for the *New York Sun* during the 1880s, and in 1923 became the editor of *Negro World*, a publication of Marcus Garvey's Universal Negro Improvement Association.

REDD FOXX

Born John Sanford in 1922, Redd Foxx was one of America's most popular comedians. He starred in the wildly popular TV show *Sanford and Son* and the television variety show *The Redd Foxx Comedy Hour*. Foxx died in 1991.

META FULLER

Meta Fuller was one of the first African-American studio sculptors. Among the first artists to employ black visual aesthetics in her portrayal of African-Americans, she was an important precursor to the Harlem Renaissance. During her career, which spanned seventy years from the 1890s until her death in 1968, she became significant for her depiction of African-American subjects.

ERNEST GAINES

Ernest Gaines was born in Oscar, Louisiana in 1933. He is the author of several books, including the critically acclaimed *Autobiography of Miss Jane Pittman* and *A Lesson Before Dying*, which won the National Book Critics Circle Award and was selected for the Oprah Winfrey Book Club in 1997. Both books have been made into television movies. He is Writer-in-Residence at the University of Southwestern Louisiana.

BOB GIBSON

Legendary pitcher Bob Gibson was born in Omaha, Nebraska. He was a sickly child, suffering from rickets and asthma. When he was a teenager, Gibson grew so quickly that he developed a heart murmur, but he played on both a YMCA team and his high school team.. He won a college scholarship that included basketball as well as baseball, and in 1957 was drafted by the Cardinals as a member of their Omaha farm club. Gibson's major league career was spent with the Cardinals until his retirement in 1977 with 251 big-league victories. After spending time as a network sportscaster and being involved with several businesses, he rejoined baseball as a coach. Gibson was inducted into the Baseball Hall of Fame in 1981.

CHARLES GILPIN

Actor Charles Sidney Gilpin won his greatest acclaim as the title character in Eugene O'Neil's *The Emperor Jones* from 1920 to 1924. He was the founder of the Lafayette Theater Company, one of the first black stock companies in New York. In 1921 he received the NAACP's Springarn Medal for his achievements.

DANNY GLOVER

Danny Glover was born in 1947 in San Francisco, California. In 1965, he enrolled in San Francisco State University, where he became affiliated with both the Black Student Union and the Black Panthers. In 1975 he became interested in acting, and by 1980 he was a prominent stage actor. His star rose in 1985, when he acted in three films, *Witness*, *Silverado*, and Steven Spielberg's *The Color Purple*. Since then he has played numerous roles, including Detective Roger Murtaugh in four *Lethal Weapon* blockbusters, and Paul D. in the film adaptation of Toni Morrison's novel *Beloved*.

MALVIN R. GOODE

Malvin Goode became the first African-American network TV reporter in 1962, at ABC-TV. In 1998, Goode was among the first African-Americans inducted into the new Hall of Fame of the National Association of Black Journalists in Washington, D.C.

WILLIAM H. GRAY III

In 1991, Congressman William H. Gray III from Pennsylvania, a Baptist preacher who had become House majority whip, gave up his seat to become President and Chief Executive Officer of the United Negro College Fund. The fund, founded in 1944, is an education assistance organization with 39 private, historically-black member colleges and universities. Since its founding, close to 300,000 men and women have graduated from college with the support of the UNCF.

DICK GREGORY

Comedian Dick Gregory made an impact in the civil rights movement by incorporating civil rights themes into his nightclub act in the 1960s. In 1968 he became the presidential nominee of the fledgling Freedom and Peace Party, a pro-civil rights and antiwar alternative political party. In addition, he was a published author of many books with racial and civil rights themes.

BRYANT GUMBEL

Bryant Gumbel began his broadcasting career in October of 1972 as a weekend sportscaster for KNBC, Los Angeles. In 1981 he was named co-anchor of the *Today* show on NBC. In 1996 he left *Today* to host a short-lived newsmagazine show, *Public Eye With Bryant Gumbel*. In 1999, Gumbel returned to early morning TV, hosting CBS' *This Morning*.

JUANITA HALL

Juanita Hall was one of the earliest African-American stage performers to reach stardom on the New York stage and to be cast in leading roles in three successful Broadway musicals. She became one of the leading black Broadway stars of the 1950s for her roles in *South Pacific* (1949), *House of Flowers* (1954) and *Flower Drum Song* (1958).

FANNY LOU HAMER

Civil rights activist Fanny Lou Hamer was a strong force behind the grass-roots organizing of the fight for equal rights in the South during the 1960s. In an effort to help black voter registration efforts, Hamer organized the Mississippi Freedom Democratic Party, a political party open to everyone, in 1964. She received many honors and awards for her efforts, including the Voter's Registration and Fight for Freedom Award in 1963, and doctoral degrees from five colleges and universities. Hamer died in 1979.

BARBARA HARRIS

Barbara Harris became the first female bishop of the Episcopal church in the United States in 1989. Her ordination broke with twenty centuries of tradition, during which only males were chosen for the highest positions in the church.

PATRICIA ROBERTS HARRIS

Patricia Roberts Harris became the Unites States' first African-American female ambassador when she was appointed by the Johnson Administration as ambassador to Luxembourg. In 1976, President Jimmy Carter appointed her secretary of Housing and Urban Development, another first for a black woman. She went on to become the secretary of Health, Education and Welfare during the Carter Administration.

WILLIAM HENRY HASTIE

With his appointment to Third Circuit Court of Appeals in 1949,

William Henry Hastie became the first African-American federal judge, a post he held until his retirement in 1971.

ROLAND HAYES

In 1917, singer Roland Hayes became the first African-American to give a concert recital at Boston's Symphony Hall. His success in the concert field broadened the opportunities for later black singers. During his career, Hayes earned many awards and citations, including the NAACP's Springarn Medal for outstanding achievement among blacks in his field.

MATTHEW HENSON

Explorer Matthew Alexander Henson became the first African-American to reach the North Pole in 1909, although there are conflicting theories whether it was Henson, or his partner, Robert Peary, who was truly the first man to accomplish this feat. When he was elected an honorary member of the Explorers Club in 1937, he became the club's first black member. Henson's autobiography, *A Negro Explorer at the North Pole*, was published in 1912.

CHESTER HIMES

Novelist Chester Himes was the creator of the famous black detective duo of Grave Digger Jones and Coffin Ed Johnson, who operated in Harlem. Nine successful novels in this series were published including *Cotton Comes to Harlem* (1965), which was made into a film in 1970. In addition, he is the writer of many successful and controversial novels containing themes of race relations and black experiences in a white world.

NATALIE HINDERAS

Internationally acclaimed pianist Natalie Hinderas was one of the first black artists to gain prominence in the field of classical music after her debut at New York City's Town Hall in 1954. She toured widely in the United States, performing with many major orchestras including the Philadelphia Orchestra, the New York Philharmonic, and the Cleveland Orchestra.

BENJAMIN HOOKS

In 1977, Benjamin Hooks, a lawyer and Baptist minister, became the executive director of the NAACP, taking over from long-time director, Roy Wilkins. One of the most influential strategies of the NAACP during the 1960s and 1970s was the concept of affirmative action, a process by which public and private employers and contractors were to ensure proportionate representation of African-Americans in the job market. By the late 1970s, this policy led to several important cases testing the concept and expressing dissatisfaction against the "reverse discrimination" features of affirmative action. During Hook's 15-year leadership, the NAACP was able to work through these issues and increase its efforts to increase black economic development by enlisting corporations to participate in Operation Fair Share.

CHARLES HAMILTON HOUSTON

Attorney and educator Charles Hamilton Houston is responsible for arguing many of the cases that set the precedent for the *Brown v. Board of Education* and *Boling v. Sharpe* cases outlawing segregation. His major impact was his work in civil rights litigation and strengthening Howard University's Law School.

RICHARD HUNT

Artist Richard Hunt is considered on the America's leading sculptors of metal. His works are on display in many major art museums in the United States including the Museum of Modern Art in New York, the Whitney Museum of American Art in New York, and the National Museum of Art in Washington, D.C.

CHARLAYNE HUNTER-GAULT

Broadcast journalist Charlayne Hunter-Gault was the first African-American woman admitted to the University of Georgia in 1961. In 1978 she joined PBS' *MacNeil/Lehrer News Hour*, becoming most familiar to viewers during her coverage of the Persian Gulf War of 1991.

SHIRLEY ANN JACKSON

Scientist Shirley Ann Jackson has made many important contributions in several areas of physics. She has worked as a visiting scientist at the European Organization for Nuclear Research in Geneva, a visiting lecturer at the NATO International Advanced Study Institute in Belgium, and has published more than 100 scientific articles and abstracts. In 1995 President Bill Clinton named Jackson chairperson of the Nuclear Regulatory Commission.

DANIEL JAMES

Daniel "Chappie" James was the first African-American to attain four-star general rank in the armed forces, and was appointed to command the North American Defense Command in 1975.

MAE JEMISON

Dr. Mae Jemison became the first African-American woman in space when she served as a science specialist aboard the space shuttle *Endeavor* in 1992.

CHARLES S. JOHNSON

In 1946, Charles Spurgeon Johnson became the first African-American president of Fisk University in Tennessee. Before serving at the university, he had served in many capacities at the National Urban League and in 1922 developed a classic study, *The Negro in Chicago: A Study of Race Relations and a Race Riot*. In addition, Johnson served on many committees and appointments of Presidents Hoover and Eisenhower.

JAMES P. JOHNSON

Pianist James P. Johnson, also a noted composer, is considered to be one of the leading exponents of New York stride piano and a major influence on the jazz pianists of his time. He is credited with some 200 compositions, many of which were written for the Broadway stage during the 1920s, his first being the musical *Runnin' Wild* (1923). Johnson collaborated with Fats Waller on the music for the Broadway revue *Keep Shufflin'* (1928), and produced *Harlem Symphony* (1932), and *Jasmine* (1934), a piano concerto. In 1940 he wrote the music for the one-act blues opera "De Organizer" with Langston Hughes.

JAMES WELDON JOHNSON

James Weldon Johnson earned great respect as a novelist, poet, songwriter, journalist, teacher, attorney, civil rights activist and diplomat. Johnson's most well known songs are "Since You Went Away" and "Lift Every Voice and Sing," considered by many as the anthem of black America. He was one of the most influential African-Americans of the early twentieth century, contributing in important ways to the development of African-American culture before, during and after the Harlem Renaissance. Johnson was a major force in the early days of the NAACP in 1916, as well as being considered one of the "elder statesmen" of the Harlem Renaissance, influencing many of the younger black writers of that era.

ROBERT L. JOHNSON

Robert L. Johnson founded Black Entertainment Television, BET, the first national cable network targeted to African-American consumers. BET Holdings, of which Johnson is the CEO, is now a multimedia entertainment company, traded on the New York Stock Exchange. In addition to BET-TV, the company has expanded into the areas African-American book publishing, jazz videos, and concerts.

VIRGINIA JOHNSON

Ballet dancer Virginia Johnson began her career as a principal dancer for Dance Theater of Harlem in 1969, a position she remained in for 20 years. She has performed as a guest artist for many major ballet companies as well as at the White House for Presidents Carter and Reagan.

SCORPIO AFRICANUS JONES

Civil rights attorney Scorpio Africanus Jones was the first black lawyer to fight a major case for the NAACP, in which he represented the defendants in the Elaine County, Arkansas race riots of 1923. As a result of winning the case, Jones saved the lives of 12 men and contributed to opening a major change in constitutional law.

JUNE JORDAN

Writer June Jordan's poetry includes: *Who Look at Me* (1969), *Some Changes* (1971), *New Days: Poems of Exile and Return* (1974), and *Naming Our Destiny: New and Selected Poems* (1989), among others. In addition, she has written children's books, two plays, numerous essays, and edited several anthologies. Jordan continues to write and teach college, and is co-founder and co-director of The Voice of the Children, Inc., a creative workshop.

PERCY LAVON JULIAN

Born in Montgomery, Alabama in 1899, Percy Lavon Julian was educated at Harvard University and received a Ph.D. from the University of Vienna. In 1936 he began to work in Chicago on research for synthesizing chemicals from soybeans. Among his breakthroughs were the synthesizing of the chemical sterol, from which the anti-arthritis medicine cortisone is derived; the drug physostigmine, which is used to treat glaucoma; and quantity production of the hormones progesterone and testosterone. An active fundraiser for the NAACP, Julian died in 1975.

ERNEST JUST

Biologist-researcher Ernest Just made major contributions in the areas of egg fertilization, artificial parthenogenesis, and cell division. His book, *The Biology of the Cell Surface*, was published in 1939.

JACOB LAWRENCE

One of the best known postwar painters, Jacob Lawrence has explored themes of African-American history and culture throughout his artistic career. In addition to teaching at Pratt Institute Art School, Art Students League and University of Washington at Seattle, his work has been exhibited at the Museum of Modern Art, the Metropolitan Museum and the Seattle Art Museum. In 1990, Lawrence was awarded the National Medal of Arts.

ROBERT H. LAWRENCE, Jr.

On June 30th, 1967, Robert H. Lawrence became the first African-American astronaut designate. He was one of four pilots chosen by the U.S. Air Force to begin training for 30-day space flights, as part of the national space program. He was killed in December of the same year in a crash during a routine proficiency flight.

JOHN ROBERT LEWIS

John R. Lewis was elected to Georgia's fifth Congressional seat in November of 1986. During his college years at Tennessee's Fisk University, Lewis helped organize the Student Nonviolent Coordinating Committee (SNCC) and became its first chairman.

ALAIN LOCKE

Born in 1886 in Philadelphia, Pennsylvania, Alain Locke was one of the major figures of the Harlem Renaissance. Locke graduated from Harvard, was a member of the Phi Beta Kappa society, and was the first black Rhodes Scholar at Oxford University in England. While teaching at Howard University in 1925, he edited the classic *The New Negro*, an anthology of African-American writings. He died on June 9, 1954, leaving a major work, *The Negro in American Culture*, unfinished.

SANDY HORACE LOVE

Inventor S. H. Love is best known for his 1933 patented design of a vending machine for bottled goods. Love was born in 1893 in Colt, Arkansas and served in Europe during World War I. During the war he developed an idea to improve military guns, for which he received a patent in 1919. In 1928 Love moved to Detroit, where he was employed by Ford Motor Company, and shortly thereafter began his design for the bottled goods vending machine. The machine featured windows for viewing selections and included a return space for empty bottles as well as dispensing a bottle deposit return coin. Although the machine was the first of its kind, Love never realized a profit on his vending machine invention. He died in 1963.

AUGUST H. MARTIN

Born in California in 1919, August Martin learned to fly in the Navy V-12 program and joined the Army Air Corps in 1945. In 1955 he was hired by Seaboard World Airlines and became the first black captain of a major U.S. commercial airline. In his spare time he flew relief missions to emerging nations. He was killed on July 1, 1968 when his plan crashed on a mission to Biafra, Africa.

JOHNNY MATHIS

From his first album, *Wonderful, Wonderful* (1956), which sold in the millions, Johnny Mathis has continued a successful recording career that has included the albums *Chances Are* (1957), *The Twelfth of Never* (1957), and *Misty* (1959).

VICTORIA EARLE MATTHEWS

Victoria Earle Matthews was the first national organizer of the National Association of Colored Women (NACW), which was founded in 1896. Known for her talent for making dramatic speeches, Matthews traveled the country encouraging respect for black women, their work, and accomplishments.

LES McCANN

Jazz pianist and singer Les McCann was a major influence on contemporary jazz. He formed his own jazz trio and released two albums in the 1960s, *Les McCann Plays the Truth* and *The Shout*. In 1970 he recorded an album at the Montreaux International Jazz Festival, *Swiss Movement*, which yielded the hit single, "Compared to What."

HATTIE McDANIEL

Hattie McDaniel became the first African-American to receive an Academy Award, which she won as best supporting actress in the 1939 film Gone with the Wind. Born in Wichita, Kansas, in 1895, she dropped out of school in 1910 to join a minstrel show. McDaniel appeared in dozens of films, including *The Little Colonel and Alice Adams* (1935), *Showboat* (1936) and *Since You Went Away* (1944).

CLAUDE McKAY

An important member of the Harlem Renaissance, Claude McKay was born in Jamaica in 1890. Educated in tradi-tional British schools, his first poetry collection, *Songs of Jamaica*, published in 1912, combined the classical style of English novels with Jamaican dialect. In 1912 McKay moved to the United States, where he attended Tuskegee Institute before transferring to Kansas State University. After two years of college; he moved to New York and immersed himself in the political life of the rising black intelligenstia, con-tributing to *The Liberator*, a leading journal of avant-garde politics and art. McKay published *Harlem Shadows* in 1922, a collection of poetry about racism, black poverty, riots, lynchings, and the character of white America.

In the late 1920s and 1930s, McKay lived abroad. His first novel, *Home to Harlem*, was published in 1928. Returning to New York, McKay wrote for magazines and newspapers, including the *New Leader* and *New Amsterdam News*. His autobiography, *A Long Way from Home* was published in 1937. He contin-ued to write about African-American city life until his death in 1948.

JOHN MERRICK

John Merrick was the founder of the North Carolina Mutual Life Insurance Company in 1898, a black-managed enterprise that achieved early financial success.

OSCAR MICHEAUX

Filmaker Oscar Micheaux formed a company in his own name (Oscar Micheaux Corp.) which made 30 films between 1919 and 1937, including *Body and Soul* (1924) in which Paul Robeson made his cinematic debut. He also wrote seven novels, which attracted a large African-American audience.

MILLS BROTHERS

Herbert (b.1912, d.1989), Harry (b. 1913, d.1982), and John (b.1911 d. 1935) were popular entertainers who worked with artists such as Bing Crosby, Louis Armstrong, Ella Fitzgerald, and Cab Calloway. Their hits included "Good-Bye, Blues," "It Don't Mean a Thing" (If it Ain't Got that Swing), and "Sixty Seconds Together."

ABBIE MITCHELL

Singer Abbie Mitchell achieved her greatest success as a concert artist, but also performed on the stage and in light comedy. Mitchell performed with many opera companies and in plays, includ-ing *Coquette* (1927), *Stevedore* (1934), and Langston Hughes' *Mulatto* (1937). In addition, she taught and headed the voice department at Tuskegee Institute in Tennessee.

ARTHUR MITCHELL

The first black premier danseur in America, Arthur Mitchell joined the New York City Ballet in 1956, becom-ing a soloist in 1959. Born in New York City in 1934, Mitchell studied in New York and appeared on Broadway and with various companies at home and abroad before joining the N.Y.C. Ballet. His most famous performances were in *Midsummer Night's Dream*, *Western Symphony* and *Afternoon of a Faun*. In 1968 Mitchell founded a ballet school in Harlem to give African-American students classical academic training. The school later became the Dance Theatre of Harlem, the first black clas-sical ballet company.

EMERSON MOORE

Emerson Moore was ordained as a Catholic priest in 1964 and was named auxiliary bishop of New York in 1982. He became a prominent figure in the case of the Howard Beach killing of a black man who was trying to escape being beaten by whites.

QUEEN MOTHER AUDLEY MOORE

Queen Mother Audley Moore has spent more than 80 years as an activist crusading for civil rights, women's rights and Pan-African nationalism. Moore organized the African-American Cultural Foundation, which fought against pejorative labels such as "Negro" and "black," and advocated the use of "African" as a more appropriate term. She also founded the World Federation of African People and the Congress of African Peoples.

GARRETT A. MORGAN

Garrett A. Morgan invented and patented the first automatic traffic light in November 1923. He had gained public attention earlier, when he invented a device he called a "Safety Hood" in 1916, used to facilitate breathing for rescue efforts during a fire or explosion. The device was picked up by the U. S. Army, who made some improvements on it; it then became the gas mask that saved thousands of lives in World War I.

BENNIE MOTEN

Bennie Moten was a legendary figure in the development of big band jazz in the lower Midwest. He spent the majority of his bandleading career in Kansas City. Moten's ensemble was one of two major swing bands in Kansas City from 1922 until his death in 1935. He began recording in the 1920s and was recognized for such releases as "Elephant Wobble/Crawdad Blues" (1923), "The New Tulsa Blues" (1927), "Moten Stomp" (1927), and "Kansas City Breakdown" (1928). In the 1930s he recorded "When I'm Alone" (1930), "Lafayette"(1932), and "Prince of Whales" (1932), among others.

CONSTANCE BAKER MOTLEY

Constance Baker Motley was named the first African-American female district judge in 1966. She had previously served as an attorney with the NAACP Legal Defense and Educational Fund, winning nine of the ten major civil rights cases she argued before the Supreme Court. When she was elected Manhattan Borough President in 1965, she became the highest-ranking elected black woman in a major American city.

JAMES MADISON NABRIT, Jr.

When attorney James Nabrit was appointed as ambassador to the United Nations in 1965, he became the highest-ranking African-American to serve in any U.S. delegation to the United Nations up to that time. Prior to that time, Nesbit had been counsel to many important civil rights cases between 1945 and 1960. His most important case was *Bolling v. Sharpe* (1954), which was one of the cases that led to the U.S. Supreme Court's declaration that public school segregation is unconstitutional.

GIL NOBLE

Television broadcaster Gil Noble is probably best known for his public affairs program, *Like It Is*, which began airing in 1968 and earned six Emmy Awards by 1980. Noble began as a correspondent for WABC-TV's *Eyewitness News* in 1967. His personal experiences, as well as some of the history of African-Americans on television, were published in his 1981 memoir *Black Is the Color of My TV Tube*.

SHAQUILLE O'NEAL

Born in Newark, New Jersey in 1972, basketball star turned actor Shaquille Rashaun O'Neal made headlines from the very start of his professional career at the age of twenty-one. O'Neal grew up on military bases, and the 7 foot 1" 300-pounder joined Louisiana State University's basketball team in 1989. After his sophomore year he was named Player of the Year by *Sports Illustrated*, A.P. and U.P.I. O'Neal left the university after his junior year and signed a contract with the Orlando Magic. His first year in the league, O'Neal was voted to the All-Star team and named 1993 Rookie of the Year. In 1996 he moved to the L.A. Lakers, was a member of the "Dream Team" for the Atlanta Olympic Games, and made his first major film. He has appeared in endorsements for Pepsi and Reebok, and has recorded and released his own rap albums, *Shaq Diesel*, *Shaq Fu: Da Return*, *The Best of Shaquille O'Neal*, *You Can't Stop The Reign*, and *Respect*.

MAJOR ROBERT OWENS

Major Robert Odell Owens was born in Memphis, Tennessee in 1936 and graduated from Morehouse College. He began his active career in public office during the civil rights movement in the 1960s. Owens was chairman of the Brooklyn Congress of Racial Equality and held several other positions in New York. In November 1982, he was elected to Congress as the representative from New York's 11th district in Brooklyn. He has been re-elected to four additional terms during which he served as a senior member of the House Committee on Education and Labor and as a member of the House Committee on Government Operations. Owens was appointed chairman of the House Subcommittee on Select Education in 1987, and served as chairman of the Congressional Black Caucus Higher Education Brain Trust from 1983 into the 1990s.

FLOYD PATTERSON

Boxer Floyd Patterson became the first person ever to regain the heavyweight championship title in boxing when he knocked out Ingemar Johansson in 1960. Patterson first gained attention in the boxing world when he won a gold medal in the middleweight competition at the 1952 Olympic Games in Helsinki, Finland. He went on to become world heavyweight champion, a title he held from 1956 to 1959, when he was knocked out by Johansson. He earned the title back a year later.

FREDERICK DOUGLAS PATTERSON

Frederick Douglas Patterson, one of America's outstanding educators, founded the United Negro College Fund in 1944. Born in Washington, D.C. in 1910, Patterson, who received Doctor of Veterinary Medicine degrees from both Iowa State and Cornell University, taught agriculture at Virginia State College between 1923 and 1928. Patterson served as Director for the School of Agriculture at Tuskeegee Institute, and then became President of Tuskeegee. He founded the only African-American veterinary school in the United States at Tuskeegee. In 1987 Patterson received the Presidential Medal of Freedom for "helping to finance excellence through America's community of historically black colleges." He died in 1988.

LINCOLN PERRY

Lincoln Theodore Monroe Andrew Perry, known as "Stepin Fetchit," is often considered to be the first African-American Hollywood star. His first movie was the 1929 all-black "talkie," *Hearts in Dixie.* Perry appeared in many films in the 1920s and 1930s, with such stars as Shirley Temple and Will Rogers, and was the first African-American to receive feature billing.

BILL PICKETT

Bill Picket, a rodeo performer during the early part of the century, gained fame for the art of bulldogging, in which he rode a steer, grabbed its horns, twisted its head back, sank his teeth into its upper lip, and wrestled it to the ground. Picket became the first African-American to be inducted into the Cowboy Hall of Fame in 1971. He died in 1932 from an injury suffered during a rodeo stunt.

WILSON PICKETT

Soul singer Wilson Pickett gained fame as a member of the Falcons, and was the group's lead singer on the 1962 hit "I Found Love." Pickett recorded the soul classics "Midnight Hour" (1965) and "Funky Broadway" (1967).

CHARLEY PRIDE

Country music singer Charley Pride was the first African-American to achieve superstar status in country and western music. His first record, "The Snakes Crawl at Night," came out in 1965, and two years later he became the first African-American to appear on Nashville's "Grand Ole Opry." Pride produced many number one hits including "All I Have to Offer You (is ME)," "Kiss an Angel Good Morning" and "Mountain of Love."

MA RAINEY

Known widely as the "Mother of the Blues," Gertrude "Ma" Rainey is generally hailed as the earliest professional blues singer. During the 1910s and 1920s, Rainey toured and sang with various circus theater groups. She began recording her music in 1923, eventually recording with many great jazz and blues musicians of the period. Some of her recordings include "Bo Weevil Blues," "Gone Daddy Blues," and "Weepin' Woman Blues."

A. PHILIP RANDOLPH

Asa Philip Randolph organized and served as first president of the first major African-American trade union when he founded the all-black International Brotherhood of Sleeping Car Porters in 1925. He held the position of president for 43 years, and was the first African-American to serve as international vice-president of the AFL-CIO, a major labor organization formed in 1955. He played a key role in organizing the historic 1963 March on Washington.

DELLA REESE

Actor and singer Della Reese began touring as a gospel singer at age 13. After achieving some success as a pop and cabaret singer, she began picking up small acting roles and in 1991 got her own television show, *The Royal Family*. She is currently starring on CBS-TV's *Touched By an Angel*.

LIONEL RICHIE

Lionel Richie began his musical career at Tuskegee University in Tennessee with the group the Commodores. The group enjoyed great success during the late 1970s with such hits as "Easy" (1977), and "Three Times a Lady" (1978). Richie left the group and began a solo career in 1982, after which he recorded many popular songs including "All Night Long," which he performed at the closing ceremonies of the 1984 Olympic Games in Los Angeles. Later that year he teamed up with Michael Jackson to write "We Are the World," which became the anthem for famine relief efforts in Ethiopia. In 1985, Richie won a Grammy Award for "Say You, Say Me," from the film *White Nights*.

MAX ROACH

Max Roach was one of key figures in the development of modern jazz, and one of the first Bebop drummers in 1943. Roach performed with his well-known quintet which, during the 1950s, included trumpeter Clifford Brown and saxophonists Sonny Rollin and Harold Land. He later became a pioneer in the use of choral backgrounds, and led his own groups of various sizes and instrumentation. Roach has been an influence on every drummer to come along since the 1940s.

FRANK ROBINSON

Frank Robinson was the first black manager in major league baseball. Robinsons talents in baseball wcrc apparent as a teenager, and he played for the the Bill Erwin Legion Post team of Oakland, California before being drafted by the Cincinnati Reds in 1956. In 1965, he was traded to the Baltimore Orioles by the Reds, who felt he was an "old thirty." By the time he retired in 1941, Robinson had received Most Valuable Player Awards in both major leagues, 586 homers, a Triple Crown, and a World Series MVP honor. He was elected to the Baseball Hall of Fame in 1982.

SMOKEY ROBINSON

William "Smokey" Robinson was born in Detroit, Michigan in 1940. At the age of 18, he formed a vocal group, which later became known as the Miracles. The group so impressed Motown owner Berry Gordy that he signed them to a recording contract in 1960.

The Miracles' first hit record for Motown was "Shop Around" (1961), an R & B song that reached number one on the *Billboard* magazine R&B charts and number two on the *Billboard* pop music charts. In the decade that followed, the Miracles produced the songs "You Really Got a Hold on Me" (1962), "Going to Go-Go" (1965), "The Tracks of My Tears" (1965), and "I Second That Emotion" (1967). In 1967 the group became known as Smokey Robinson and the Miracles. During the 1960s Robinson also wrote and produced classics for other Motown artists. "My Girl" was written for the Temptations, "You Beat Me to the Punch" (1962) and "My Guy" (1964) were written for Mary Wells, and he wrote "Ain't That Peculiar" (1965) for Marvin Gaye.

Robinson left the Miracles in 1972 to pursue a solo music career, and his other notable hits included "Being with You" (1981) and "Just to See Her" (1987), which won a Grammy Award in 1988. In 1990, Robinson won a Grammy Legends Award. He was inducted into the Rock and Roll Hall of Fame in 1987.

CARL ROWAN

Carl Rowan became one of the first 15 African-Americans to earn a commission in the U.S. Navy in 1944. He was named deputy assistant secretary for public affairs for the U. S. Department of State in 1963, and in 1963 became U. S. ambassador to Finland. In addition, he had a long-running column in the *Chicago Sun* and has published several books. Rowan's memoir, *Breaking Barriers*, was published in 1991.

DIANA SANDS

Actress Diana Sands got her first break in Lorraine Hansberry's 1959 Broadway play, *Raisin in the Sun*. Sands recreated her role of Beneatha Younger for the film version two years later, and continued a film career that lasted through the 1960s and into the 1970s. Her films include *Ensign Pulver* (1964), *The Landlord* (1970), *Doctor's Wives* (1971), and *Honey-baby, Honeybaby* (1974), among others. Sands has appeared on Broadway and made many television guest appearances throughout her acting career as well.

AUGUSTA SAVAGE

Sculptor Augusta Savage gained fame for her exploration of black subjects in works such as *Gamin* (1929), *Woman of Martinique* (1932), and *The Harp* (1939). She was an active teacher for years in private classes and community studios, particularly under the Works Progress Administration. Savage's works were exhibited at the Schomberg Center in 1988 and 1989.

NTOZAKE SHANGE

Ntozake Shange's play, *For Colored Girls Who Have Considered Suicide When the Rainbow is Enuf*, was first produced in California in 1976. The play went on to New York where it had a long run, earning Tony, Grammy and Emmy Award nominations in 1977. Shange has produced many works for the stage as well as books. In 1981 she received an Obie award for her play *Mother Courage and Her Children*. The Broadway version of *For Colored Girls* was revived in 1995.

CHARLIE SIFFORD

In 1961, Charlie Sifford became the first African-American golfer to play full-time with the Professional Golfers Association (PGA) tour. Sifford played on the PGA circuit for 15 years and became a regular on the Senior PGA tour after it was instituted in 1980. His autobiography, *Just Let Me Play*, was published in 1992.

NINA SIMONE

Singer and pianist/organist Nina Simone became involved with the civil rights movement of the 1960s and integrated black pride and other social themes into her music. An eclectic vocalist, Simone recorded compositions ranging from blues and jazz to soul. Some of her better known recordings are, "Ain't Got No—I Got Life" from Hair, and "To Love Somebody." Simone's albums include *Nina Simone Plays the Blues* and *Here Comes the Sun*, issued between 1967 and 1972; *Baltimore* (1978); and *Let It Be Me* (1987).

NOBLE SISSLE

Noble Sissle teamed up with Eubie Blake to write and direct the first all-black musical of the 1920s, *Shuffle Along*. *Shuffle Along* opened in May 1921 at New York City's Sixty-Third Street Theater, where it became so popular that crowds gathered on the sidewalk waiting to buy tickets, while cars and taxicabs jammed the streets. After a record 504 performances on Broadway, *Shuffle Along* went on the road to play for two more years.

CHARLES C. SPAULDING

In 1923, Charles C. Spaulding was appointed president of the North Carolina Mutual Insurance Company. Under Spaulding, the company became one of the most successful black-owned businesses in American history, with more than $200 million in assets in 1992. Spaulding had previously been vice president of the Mutual, and was a pioneer in saturation advertising, making sure that local businesses had plenty of matchbooks, calendars and pens advertising his company.

MABEL K. STAUPERS

Nursing executive Mabel Keaton Staupers served as executive secretary of the Harlem Committee of the New York Tuberculosis and Health Association from 1922 to 1934, before accepting the same position at the National Association of Colored Graduate Nurses (NACGN)—an organization that worked to improve working conditions for African-American nurses. During World War II, with the help of First Lady Eleanor Roosevelt, Staupers fought to integrate in the U. S. Armed Forces for African-American nurses who wished to serve their country. By the end of the war both the U.S. Army and the U.S. Navy Nurse Corps were integrated.

JOHN STEPTOE

John Steptoe's first book, *Stevie*—written when he was 19 years old—was named an ALA Notable Children's Book and won the Society of Illustrators Gold Medal. In 1988, his African tale, *Mufaro's Beautiful Daughters* (1987) won the Coretta Scott King Award and was named a Caldecott Honor Book. Among his other popular children's books are *Uptown, Trainride,* and *The Story of Jumping Mouse: A Native American Legend* (1985), which was named a Caldecott Honor Book.

BILLY TAYLOR

Pianist and composer Billy Taylor has earned a Peabody Award for his work during the 1950s and 1960s organizing and hosting programs on television and radio about jazz music. From 1968 to 1972, Taylor led an 11-piece band for television's *David Frost Show.* In the late 1970s to early 1980s, he directed *Jazz Alive!* for National Public Radio (NPR). Taylor has been a regular on CBS *Sunday Morning* since 1980, serving as the program's jazz correspondent, and earning an Emmy Award in 1983 for a segment on Quincy Jones.

DEBI THOMAS

Debi Thomas was the winner at the 1985 National Sports Festival in Baton Rouge, Louisiana. In 1986 she captured the U.S. and World figure skating titles, becoming the first African-American to capture an international singles meet. At the 1988 Olympics in Calgary, Canada, Thomas won the bronze medal in women's singles. During the time she was competing, Thomas was also a pre-med major at Stanford University. She retired from amateur competition after the 1988 Olympics to complete her undergraduate studies, and began making professional appearances. In 1992, Thomas retired from professional competition to attend medical school.

WILLIAM MONROE TROTTER

William Monroe Trotter earned both his bachelor's and master's degrees from Harvard University, and was the first African-American student at the university to be elected to Phi Beta Kappa. In 1901, at the age of 29, Trotter founded the *Boston Guardian,* a newspaper devoted to equal rights for African-Americans. In addition, Trotter was founder and secretary of the National Equal Rights League, an activist civil rights group.

MELVIN VAN PEEBLES

Actor and director Melvin Van Peebles made a string of films in the late 1960s and early 1970s, including *Story of a Three Day Pass* (1967), *Watermelon Man* (1970), and *Sweet Sweetback's Baadasssss Song* (1971). The extraordinary success of *Sweet Sweetback's Baadasssss Song,* which grossed nearly $14 million dollars, began a new era for black directors in the movie industry and paved the way for future directors, such as Spike Lee. In 1971 and 1972, Van Peebles directed two Broadway plays, *Aint' Supposed to Die a Natural Death* and *Don't Play Us Cheap.* Throughout the 1970s and 1980s, Van Peebles continued to write and direct for films, plays and television. In the 1990s, he began working as a team with his son, Mario, on a variety of projects, including *Panther,* a fictionalized movie of the history of The Black Panthers.

DIONNE WARWICK

Singer Dionne Warwick became well known for her recordings of songs by composer Burt Bacharach, many of which reached the top ten in the 1960s and 1970s. Her first number one hit, "Then Came You" (1974), was recorded with the Spinners. Warwick had a number of successful albums in the late 1970s and early 1980s, and recorded the hit "I'll Never Love This Way Again" in 1979.

MAXINE WATERS

Maxine Waters was elected to the California State Assembly in 1976, where she served on various committees until she was elected to the U.S. House of Representatives in 1990. She is a outspoken advocate for minorities and the poor and has fought for legislation promoting aid to poor and minority neighborhoods in urban areas. Waters serves on the board of *Essence* magazine and is involved in the National Women's Caucus as well as the National Steering Committee on Education of Black Youth. In 1996 Waters won an Essence Award for her work.

BARBARA WATSON

Barbara Watson became the first African-American to achieve the rank of Assistant Secretary of State when President Johnson appointed her Assistant Secretary of State for Consular Affairs in 1968. She served the position under Presidents Johnson, Nixon, Ford and Carter.

L. DOUGLAS WILDER

L. Douglas Wilder became the first African-American elected to the Virginia senate since 1869. He served five terms in the state senate and achieved another political first in 1985 when he won the lieutenant governorship. Four years later Wilder was the first African-American to be elected governor when he became Virginia's governor. In 1991, Wilder launched a presidential campaign on the Democratic ticket, but withdrew his bid four months later.

PAUL R. WILLIAMS

Known as the "architect to the stars," Paul R. Williams designed hundreds of homes in areas such as Beverly Hills and Bel Air, California, including those of entertainers Cary Grant, Frank Sinatra, Lucille Ball, and Danny Thomas. In addition, he designed the Los Angeles County Courthouse, the mansion in Pasedena used in the *Batman* television series, and a number of landmark buildings in the African-American communities of Los Angeles. Williams was the first African-American member of the American Institute of Architects.

BERT WILLIAMS

In 1903, comedian Bert Williams and his partner, George Williams presented *In Dahomey*, the first full-length Broadway musical written and performed by African-Americans. Williams became popular as a solo performer, starring in 1909 in another all-black show, *Mr. Lode of Koal*. When he was featured in the *Ziegfield Follies*, Williams became the first African-American performer to star in a white show. He performed in Follies until 1919. Williams died suddenly in 1922, at the age of 49.

DANIEL HALE WILLIAMS

In 1891, Dr. Daniel Hale Williams founded Provident Hospital in Chicago, the first hospital in the country with an interracial staff. Williams became famous throughout the country for his skill and innovative techniques as a surgeon.

SHIRLEY ANNE WILLIAMS

Shirley Anne Williams was born in Bakersfield, California in 1945. Williams attended Fresno State University and earned a master's degree in American literature from Brown University. A celebrated poet and author, Williams won many awards throughout her life, including an Emmy Award for a television performance of her poetry, and the ALA Caldecott Award and Coretta Scott King Book Award for *Working Cotton* (1992). Her other books were nominated for a Pulitzer Prize and two National Book Awards. Williams died of cancer in 1999.

LOUIS TOMPKINS WRIGHT

In 1919 Louis T. Wright became the first African-American doctor on the staff of New York's Harlem Hospital. Three years later he became the hospital's director of surgery. In 1928 Wright was made the first African-American police surgeon in the history of the New York City Police Department. While serving the police department, he invented a brace for patients with neck fractures that is still used today. Wright founded the Harlem Hospital Cancer Research Foundation in 1948.

INDEX

PHOTO CREDITS